THE COLLISION 4

A Year of Cultural Conversations &
Spiritual Collisions

THE COLLISION VOLUME FOUR
A Year of Cultural Conversations & Spiritual Collisions

Published by Blackaby Minitries International
P.O Box 1035
Jonesboro, GA 30237
Blackaby.org

Printed in the United States of America

2021–1st ed

Cover design, interior design and typeset: Joni Le

All Scripture quotations, unless otherwise indicated, are taken from the Holy Bible, New International Version®, NIV®. Copyright ©1973, 1978, 1984, 2011 by Biblica, Inc.™ Used by permission of Zondervan. All rights reserved worldwide. www.zondervan.com. The "NIV" and "New International Version" are trademarks registered in the United States Patent and Trademark Office by Biblica, Inc.™

This publication uses Scripture quotations from the ESV® Bible (The Holy Bible, English Standard Version®), Copyright © 2001 by Crossway, a publishing ministry of Good News Publishers. Used by permission. All rights reserved.

This publication uses Scripture quotations from the Holy Bible, New Living Translation, copyright ©1996, 2004, 2015 by Tyndale House Foundation. Used by permission of Tyndale House Publishers, Carol Stream, Illinois 60188. All rights reserved.

ISBN 978-1-7350872-9-0

Table of Contents

REVIEWS

Introduction

This is a book about Christian cultural engagement. After the turmoil of the last few years, it is crucial for Christians to stay engaged with culture. What has also become clear is that "cultural engagement" is a loaded term.

The buzz phrase has become popular within the church as Christians seek to live in accordance with Jesus' prayer for his followers to be "in the world" but "not of the world" **(John 17)**. Christians are pilgrims in a world that is not our true home, living among people who have not yet experienced spiritual rebirth. Therefore, tension and disagreement are inevitable. How we navigate that friction is important.

Language is always in flux. Against a backdrop of widespread cultural division and polarization, the word "engage" has frequently adopted the stigma of war language. We "engage" our opposition on the field of battle. We caution our friends not to "engage" with trolls on social media, with the understanding that "engagement" of that sort is synonymous with "conflict." So when we speak of "cultural engagement," what do we actually mean?

Perhaps a better understanding of cultural engagement is presence. When Jesus prayed for his disciples, he did not relay specific instructions for how they should be actively "in the world." The one clear implication is that Jesus' disciples were to be in the world. How might that look today?

The "war" language may not always be inappropriate. As secular culture perpetuates ungodly ideologies, challenges biblical teaching, and flaunts its sinful rebellion, one aspect of Christians' calling to be "present" is to push back against these sinful trends. At the same time, Christians should avoid becoming cultural warmongers. If our default posture is cultural warfare, then we should examine our hearts in light of Jesus' blessing, "Blessed are the peacemakers, for they will be called children of God" **(Matthew 5:9)**.

Jesus also lived in an ungodly pagan society. He certainly stood firm for truth and challenged misguided teaching and behavior. Yet he was not known as a cultural revolutionary or warrior but as a "friend of sinners" **(Luke 7:34)**. Jesus vexed the religious leaders with his habit of being present in areas of culture that were unexpected, uncomfortable, and hostile.

Pop culture is the arena in which many of today's important cultural conversations are taking place. It is an area in desperate need of Christian presence. The world does not need Christians in conflict with culture as much as it requires Christians in conversation with it. The Christian voice must be heard in these cultural conversations, not merely as a shout of condemnation but as an active participant in an unfolding dialogue. Christians can be active members of this world, even as we are citizens of another. We can listen as well as talk. We can hear the stories told all around us, even as we fulfill our mission to proclaim the gospel as the greatest story ever told.

In short, Christians should be culturally engaged not just as warriors but as conversationalists. After all, culture is not our enemy; it is our mission field. Christians do not seek to conquer society but to spread a gospel of love that promises liberty.

About This Book

This book is an embodiment of the mission described above. As with the previous volumes in this anthology series, the following pages contain examples of Christian engagement in various cultural conversations. Some of the articles explore general principals and frameworks. Others are directed toward specific cultural moments. In each of these chapters—the general and the topical—we hope you will see past the specific conversation and recognize the methods and approaches with which to engage in those conversations.

You are welcome to read through this book chronologically or to jump around and explore the chapters that most interest you. The topics change from year to year (and even day to day), but the need for Christians to be active participants in the dialogue remains unchanged. In whichever way you choose to approach this book, our prayer is that you will be inspired and challenged to engage thoughtfully and purposefully with the culture around you.

About the Collision

The Collision is a digital, multi-media platform aimed at equipping Christians to navigate the inevitable collisions between Christ and culture. Through online articles, YouTube videos, books, podcasts, livestreams, newsletters, and social media, The Collision cultivates honest cultural conversations about the important issues Christians face today and encourages believers to collide with the world for Christ.

We hope you will consider joining our community of culturally engaged Christians from around the world as together we seek to collide with the world for Christ.

Join the movement by connecting with us online:

- Website: thecollision.org
- YouTube: Youtube.com/c/thecollisionbmi
- Facebook: @Thecollisionbmi
- Twitter: @Thecollisionbmi

Entertainment and Christian Liberty

How far does Christian liberty extend?

For many Christians, it reaches far and wide but ultimately stops on the doorstep of Hollywood. Beyond that threshold, in the dystopian landscape of the arts and entertainment industry, legalism still reigns supreme.

I should point out that legalism doesn't mean holding steadfastly to biblical teachings. Rather, legalism adds "fine print" to those commands and then militantly enforces them using God's authority to judge others against a man-made standard. Entertainment is fertile soil for this type of legalism to sprout.

A legalistic mindset arises most often in gray areas, and arguably nothing is murkier than art and entertainment. The issue is complicated by the fact that scripture remains largely silent on entertainment choices. The Bible tells us to love God, love our neighbor, be holy, and make

disciples. It does *not* spell out how those commands relate to watching comic book movies, listening to heavy metal, or reading popular novels. Scripture offers several general principles, but knowing how to apply them can be difficult and often contentious. Where no clearly defined rules exist, we are prone to creating our own (no R-rated movies, no "secular" music, no fantasy stories containing "magic," etc.).

In recent days, films such as Pixar's controversial *Turning Red*, magic-filled Harry Potter films, and the mysticism of *Dune* have caused much debate within the church about Christian entertainment choices. The discourse frequently goes beyond personal convictions and becomes a public adjudication that *no* Christian should engage with certain works.

What is striking about these discussions is that despite the disagreements, the framework remains primarily legalistic, people bickering about where to draw the lines of acceptable Christian behavior. An important element of the debate that is often overlooked is "liberty." There are at least three important ways Christian liberty should influence our approach to entertainment.

1. All Things Are Lawful

When making entertainment choices, Christians often start from a posture of condemnation and then work outward toward what is permissible:

"Can Christians watch R-rated movies?"

"Is it appropriate for Christians to play violent video games?"

"Can you be a Christian and play Dungeons & Dragons?"

These questions imply that all entertainment is junk food, and we must discern how much we can get away with without feeling shame for cheating on our diet plan.

The Early Church inverted this paradigm. The Apostle Paul wrote, "'All things are lawful,' but not all things are helpful. 'All things are lawful,' but not all things build up. Let no one seek his own good, but the good of his neighbor" **(1 Corinthians 10:23-24)**. Paul's teaching about how Christians should navigate divisive cultural issues (e.g. eating meat sacrificed to idols) was to start from a position of utmost freedom and then to work *backwards*, eliminating anything that was detrimental to one's faith or to the health of the church.

Christian liberty requires prudent choices rather than rule following.

When making entertainment choices today, Christians can start from a position of liberty rather than legalism. The Bible may condemn a secular worldview embedded within a popular film, but it doesn't prohibit Christians from watching movies containing secular worldviews. In fact, there may be good reasons to watch them—to understand the world, to gain a new perspective, or simply because it's a well-crafted, excellently made film. At the same time, a Christian may discern that viewing the movie is unwise and elect *not* to watch it. Christian liberty requires prudent choices rather than rule following. We are no longer bound to a restrictive, shame-inducing diet plan, but we would still do well to eat healthy foods and avoid that third Krispy Kreme doughnut.

2. Abusing Liberty

When a Jailor tells a prisoner, "You're free," he doesn't mean the ex-convict is free to do *anything*. Likewise, there are always two sides to freedom in scripture:

"Act as free men, and do not use your freedom as a covering for evil, but use it as bondslaves of God" **(1 Peter 2: 16)**.

"For you were called to freedom, brethren; only do not turn your freedom into an opportunity for the flesh, but through love serve one another" **(Galatians 5:13)**.

Christians haven't been set free to fill our hearts and minds with entertainment that glorifies the same sin and moral filth from which we have been liberated. Christian liberty is not a free pass to embrace a reckless, "anything goes" attitude. Christians have been set free, but we have also been called to "be holy" **(1 Peter 1: 15-16)**. Christians have liberty, but also a mandate to love our neighbor **(Mark 12:31)**. These callings should lead Christians to navigate entertainment choices differently than the unbelieving world does. We may temporarily need to set aside our liberty for the good of others.

3. Charity & Conversations

A comment posted on a recent movie review reflects an often-forgotten aspect of this discussion: charity.

"@The Collision: if you follow the word of God, then you know there is only one Christian perspective."

This statement conflates the existence of one true gospel with one true Christian perspective. There is only one path to salvation, and sin is sin. On these essential salvific issues, there is no alternative perspective. But even Paul and

Diversity of perspectives within the church is one of its most valuable characteristics. Christians should have thoughtful conversations about complicated issues such as entertainment choices.

Peter clashed over important church issues. Paul and Barnabas "had such a sharp disagreement that they parted company" **(Acts 15: 39)**. At the Jerusalem Council, Paul argued that gentile converts didn't require circumcision **(Acts 15)**, but in the next chapter he has his pupil Timothy circumcised **(Acts 16:3)**. Was it appropriate for believers to eat meat that had been sacrificed to idols? Yes and no **(1 Corinthians 8)**.

Regarding salvation in Christ alone, the church was of one mind. But there has always been differing perspectives and convictions on how best to live as Christians in culture. Steadfastly believing in one true gospel does not mean having a unified perspective on *all* matters.

Whenever a Christian claims there is only one true "Christian" perspective on an issue, that "right" perspective is inevitably their own. In that, we are like the first-century pharisees who were so confident that they alone had cracked the code and deciphered the correct answer to every religious question that they refused to listen to anyone else—including the Son of God.

Diversity of perspectives within the church is one of its most valuable characteristics. Christians should have thoughtful conversations about complicated issues such as entertainment choices. Christians should share their convictions and be willing to listen to other perspectives. If Christians are concerned about the influence certain entertainment choices are having on another believer, they should express their concern with grace and charity.

If someone making different entertainment choices causes us to question that person's salvation, then we have embraced a works-based legalism, not the true gospel. The Christian gospel isn't, "Believe in your heart, profess Jesus as Lord, don't watch R-rated movies, and you will be saved." Christians can agree on the gospel and disagree on what to watch on Netflix.

When it comes to living together as the church, it has been wisely said, "In essentials unity, in non-essentials liberty, in all things charity."

How Children's Entertainment Became an Ideological Battle- ground

"Hollywood is coming for our kids."

That refrain, or some variation of it, has become an increasingly popular rallying cry in recent years. Whereas entertainment aimed toward children was perhaps once viewed as a diverting babysitter, these movies and TV shows now seem motivated to educate and disseminate ideologies.

Many parents explain the current undesirable state of children's entertainment with the simple assertion, "Hollywood is run by a bunch of perverts who want to corrupt kids." In one sense, Hollywood has always been obsessed with sex. The entertainment industry has continually pushed boundaries, probing current and potential social norms. But it hits differently when children are involved. The question is, why now? Why does it seem like children's entertainment has become a battleground?

There are rarely simple answers to complicated questions. Perhaps the issue here is less about a group of shady perverts playing cards in a smoke-filled room and brainstorming how to sexualize children and more of a reflection of our shifting concept of entertainment audiences. Children's entertainment is becoming an ideological battleground because the very concept of children's entertainment is rapidly vanishing.

The Disappearance of Childhood

In a recent interview, Disney CEO Bob Chapek said, "I always say that once our fans and audiences put their kids to bed at night after watching *Pinocchio* or *Dumbo* or *The Little Mermaid*, they are probably not gonna tune into another animated movie. They want something for them."

The quote sparked instant backlash and widespread scorn across social media. The prevailing objection can be summed up by esteemed director Guillermo del Toro, "Animation is not a genre for kids; it's a medium. Animation is film. Animation is art. And it can tell stories that are gorgeous and complex that feel handmade by humans for humans." Although commenting on a specific situation, del Toro's response reflects the fading boundaries of demographically divided audiences.

In 1982, cultural prophet Neil Postman published an insightful book called *The Disappearance of Childhood*. In it, he argued that the innovation of television would inevitably erode the traditional distinctions between adulthood and childhood. Unlike books, which have the built-in gatekeeping mechanism of required literacy, the visual medium of television is accessible to all ages. Postman's insights have proven correct. Additionally, the internet has accelerated the demographic dissolve by making visual entertainment instantly accessible. The same streaming platform that offers "kid-friendly" animated films also houses mature "adult" content, which contains violent, sexual material.

Adult Themes for Children

The blurring of demographic lines, coupled with the increased commercialization of entertainment, has had a trickle-down effect on content creation. Gone is the Loony Tunes era when cartoon characters amused kids by dropping an anvil on an anthropomorphic coyote. Part of this shift can be called the "Pixar Effect." Previously, children's films sought to appeal to adults by simply tossing in a handful of crude innuendos that went over children's heads. In contrast, Pixar Studios sought to make animated films that adults could enjoy unironically. *UP* (2009) is a fun, emotionally satisfying film whether you are 6 or 60. In del Toro's words, it is a film aimed at humans, not just kids.

The inherent problem with telling universal human stories rather than age-specific ones, however, is that not all material is appropriate for all ages. One of the most controversial films of the year is Pixar's *Turning Red*. The story deals primarily with puberty and menstruation. Animation may not be solely for children, but a colorful animated film about a fluffy red panda is likely to appeal most to an audience that won't experience puberty for years.

It introduces sexuality to non-sexual beings and then teaches them how to navigate it, creating a demand to supply.

Thus, while potentially helping older children and teens navigate the universal human rite of puberty, it also gives younger children answers to questions they likely didn't even know to ask. It introduces sexuality to non-sexual beings and then teaches them how to navigate it, creating a demand to supply.

The complication also flows in the other direction. It's not just that "children's entertainment" is aiming higher but also that adult entertainment is shooting lower. For example, adults and children alike enjoy the superhero genre. This mutual fandom sets the stage for some equally thorny storytelling decisions.

Jessica Gao, creator of the Disney+ original show *She-Hulk*, recently made headlines for declaring her intention to make a "sex-positive" show that appeals to children: "We wanted to make it realistic, and about a woman navigating sex, but also make it something that everybody can enjoy, including children, because there is an element of the show that is really fun for young people." Commercial motivations have pushed movie studios to desire the widest possible audience (including children) for their blockbuster properties, while creative interests have compelled storytellers to explore adult themes and experiences.

Marvel's *The Eternals* was heralded for featuring the first on-screen sex scene in the MCU. The film's director, Chloé Zhao, explained, "To have a sex scene that will be seen by a lot of people that shows their love and compassion and gentleness—I think it's a really beautiful thing." The simultaneous desires to push the boundaries and to invite the largest possible audience are on an inevitable collision course.

The New Normal

If there is a problem, it is not necessarily that Hollywood storytellers want to explore sex or other adult themes. Christians are wise to filter these stories through a biblical worldview, but the experiences and themes themselves are valid material for cinematic exploration. Not every story needs to be "family friendly." It is appropriate for adults to have stories that explore adult issues, just as it is useful for children to have entertainment that presents childhood experiences. The bigger issue is that the entertainment industry is losing its traditional audience distinctions, making it difficult to know which is which. Also, once adult themes have become the norm in animated films, the doors are open for creators to push agendas that would previously have been impossible.

The solution is not necessarily to return to the days when children's entertainment was a mere sugar

The days when parents could basically trust every animated film to restrict itself to children's themes and material is long gone.

rush of loud diversion that made parents pull their hair out. Kids can handle more than that, and there are universal stories that can in-deed be enjoyed across demographics. But the days when parents could basically trust every animated film to restrict itself to children's themes and material is long gone. Parents need to be aware and stay educated.

Part of that awareness is understanding that the issue goes deeper than a group of sexually motivated storytellers with an agenda. Hollywood creatives did not just wake up one morning with the sudden desire to go after the hearts and minds of children. Rather, the ideological battleground of children's entertainment is the by product of an entertainment industry that has been slowly shifting for decades.

Beyond Condemnation: Why Christians Should Engage with Disagreeable Movies

Hollywood is many things—some good, some bad. In its purest form, it's an arena for storytelling. Cinema is where many of today's significant cultural conversations take place, where important issues are explored, debated, affirmed, challenged, and deconstructed.

Christians, commissioned to be present in the culture around us, should engage with these stories. Unfortunately, "engagement" is not always the best word to describe the church's interaction with Hollywood's narratives. Christians "navigate" them like a ship captain adrift amongst tumultuous waters; we critique them or condemn them, but we don't always engage with them.

One reason for this lack of engagement is simply that many of us don't watch films that require much engagement. There's a misconception that we should not expose ourselves to movies that embody disagreeable ideologies, content, or themes. Doing so is not only deemed unwise but inherently sinful. Many Christians tend to decide the "appropriateness" of a film based on how closely it aligns with our religious convictions and values. This guiding principle results in a simple accept/reject dichotomy. If it affirms Christian beliefs, we give it a stamp of approval. If it challenges or opposes those beliefs, we reject and condemn it.

What's missing is a willingness to *engage* with these "disagreeable" movies and the cultural conversations they inspire.

"Is it Biblical?"

When I review movies, people often ask, "Is it biblical?" The underlying concern is typically whether the worldviews, content, messages, or themes the film depicts are consistent with what the Bible teaches about Christian behavior and living. Are the characters good role models? Does their lifestyle or worldview align with scripture?

The Bible describes the Christian life, but that is just one part of its story. Scripture is filled with inspiring saints, but also wretched sinners (and it reveals how those saints *are* sinners). The gospel is the story of humanity's salvation, but also our depravity and need for a savior. In other words, the Bible is not escapist literature; it's a raw, brutally honest revelation of how God is alive and at work amidst a sinful and fallen world. As Christians today, we can sometimes become squeamish about viewing the world with the same unfiltered truthfulness.

Holy and Discerning

To be clear, "disagreeable" does not mean morally compromising. We're not talking about movies filled with explicit sex scenes, relentlessly profane language, and gratuitous violence ("Watching trashy Netflix shows for Jesus!").

Jesus said, "I am sending you out like sheep among wolves. Therefore be as shrewd as snakes and as innocent as doves" **(Matthew 10:16)**. Christians are called to be holy just as God is holy **(1 Peter 1:15-16)**, and that encompasses our time in a movie theater or binging Hulu. But encountering opposing worldviews

and ideologies is not necessarily an assault on Christian holiness. We should be holy and discerning, but also thinking and engaged.

A Bible verse Christians often cite to oppose such thinking is **Philippians 4:8**: "Finally, brothers and sisters, whatever is true, whatever is noble, whatever is right, whatever is pure, whatever is lovely, whatever is admirable—if anything is excellent or praiseworthy—think about such things."

This passage is foundational to Christian cultural engagement, but it can be easily misused. Paul did not avoid all opposing ideologies and worldviews. His teaching to "think about such things" did not conflict with his willingness to engage with the pagan Greek poems and narratives or the visual imagery of false gods and spirituality that permeated his culture **(Acts 17)**.

The mentality that Christians should never expose ourselves to stories with which we disagree sounds pious but can actually be a cover for intellectual laziness. If a belief must be guarded against any exposure to alternative thinking, then it is a dangerously fragile belief.

Christians often claim that disagreeable entertainment is

"planting seeds," a reference to the Parable of the Sower **(Matthew 13)**. But when Jesus told the parable, the emphasis was on the soil, not the seeds. When it comes to engaging entertainment, Christians should focus more on the soil and less on the seeds. We ought to remain anchored in **Philippians 4:8**, not as an escape into soft, unchallenging content but as a way to engage with opposing ideologies.

Engaging Stories

Christians don't need to see the gospel in every movie, but we should view each film through the lens of the gospel. Rather than rigidly ensuring all the entertainment we consume perfectly aligns with our faith, we should take our faith into each experience.

Many disagreeable movies are "excellent" from a craftsmanship standpoint and "true" insofar as the stories are authentic expressions of the real, sinful world. Should Christians model their life on each of the characters or always agree with the filmmaker's perspective? Of course not. But I don't watch Hollywood films to learn how to live the Christian life. I read the Bible and go to church for that. I watch movies to hear the stories of the day and to engage with the cultural conversations they spark. Watching does not equal endorsement. It's not a sin to listen and seek to understand another perspective or worldview. Movies are a window into the world and the people who live in it.

There are important cultural conversations happening through movies and entertainment. Christians aren't obligated to consume filth, and we are certainly not required to agree with the perspective presented in every movie. But we should be willing to join the dialogues happening in our culture. After all, Christians have much to contribute to these conversations.

How Movies Influence Us (and What Christians Should Do About It)

Actor Diego Luna once said, "Cinema is a mirror that can change the world." His statement captures the complex, circular relationship between cinema and reality. Movies reflect the landscape in which we live today, while also shaping the world we will experience tomorrow.

There is little question that movies influence people on both a societal and individual level. The trickier discussion is *how*. Christians have been invested in this idea for as long as movies have existed, but the issue has become increasingly relevant to the wider culture.

Many people today seem to believe filmmakers are morally obligated to use their influence to shape society. The Brady Center to Prevent Gun Violence, in cooperation with prominent Hollywood creatives J. J. Abrams, Judd Apatow, Damon Lindelof, Mark Ruffalo, Jimmy Kimmel, and many others recently released an open letter that included the following declaration:

"As America's storytellers, our goal is primarily to entertain, but we also acknowledge that stories have the power to effect change. Cultural attitudes toward smoking, drunk driving, seatbelts and marriage equality have all evolved due in large part to movies' and TV's influence. It's time to take on gun safety."

Preceding that quote is the curious statement, "We didn't cause the problem, but we want to help fix it." While Christians typically view the power of film as largely negative, secular culture embraces it in a positive, almost salvific sense. Yet, for better or worse, there is agreement that movies *do* influence us.

More Than Messages

Much of the Christian discourse surrounding the influence of entertainment focuses on a film's message but overlooks the fact that cinema is largely an emotional artform. Audiences choose which movies to watch predominantly based on which emotions we want to arouse. We watch horror to experience fear, adventure to feel exhilarated, or rom-coms to make us happy.

In the book *Moving Viewers: American Film and the Spectator's Experience*, film scholar Carl Plantinga puts it this way:

"In the analysis of films and literature, traditional interpretation searches for hidden meaning, as though each work of fiction embodies abstract propositions in the form of messages or themes," but "any abstract meaning that a film might have is ancillary to the experience in which that meaning is embodied" (3).

In simpler terms, the ideology or message a film presents is only as powerful as its emotional packaging. Movies influence us most not by making us think something but by causing us to *feel* a certain way and allowing those feelings to shape our thinking. Biblical wisdom affirms this idea: "Above all else, guard your heart, for everything you do flows from it" **(Proverbs 4:23)**.

Emotional Impact

Christians engaging with entertainment typically focus on recognizing the secular ideologies Hollywood films depict. This component is important, and Christians certainly should be cognizant of the worldviews and messages films are spreading.

That said, many of the messages that outrage Christians the most, because they are so easily recognized, are probably not much of an actual threat. Someone screaming, "THERE IS NO GOD" is only a challenge to shallow faith. When ideologies are presented on a rational, intellectual level, we can engage with them in a like manner. More influential is the way films can shape our emotions toward those ideologies.

A recent example is the discussion surrounding Pixar's *Lightyear* and its controversial LGBTQ subplot. In an interview, actor Chris Evans explained, "The goal is that we can get to the point where it is the norm, and that this doesn't have to be some uncharted waters, that eventually this is just the way it is. That representation across the board is how we make films." The movie attempts to normalize same-sex relationships not through a clear or upfront "message" but simply by presenting one as a touching, emotional love story.

A Christian Response

Given movies' emotional power, how should Christians respond? To start, Christians should avoid thinking either too much or too little about films' power. Some Christians vastly overstate the persuasive influence of movies, as though viewers are like Anakin Skywalker powerlessly being pulled to the Dark Side. On the other hand, it would be foolish and arrogant to assume films don't influence us. Our sinful human hearts are not impenetrable. Hollywood recognizes the power it wields through cinematic storytelling, and Christians are wise to do likewise.

Understanding entertainment's emotional power should inform the way we engage with it. We should be aware of the worldviews embedded within a film, but we should avoid reducing a movie to its worldview. Rather, we should pay as much attention to the medium as to the message. We should consider not only *what* the film says but *how* it says it. Blatant secular ideologies are easy to recognize and reject. Far

greater discernment is required to engage with the subtle emotional responses that wash over us, often undetected.

Christians need not fear Hollywood films, but we shouldn't be careless either. Movies are a powerful vehicle for change, and such change comes most often through our emotions. Hollywood recognizes this reality. Christians would be foolish to ignore it.

"Why So Dark?" A Christian Perspective on Dark Storytelling

In Christopher Nolan's *The Dark Knight*, the Joker famously muses, "Why so serious?" When considering the current slate of fantastical storytelling in many popular films and books today, we might similarly ask, "Why so dark?"

The fantasy genre has always contained dark themes and violence. Those who dismiss fantasy as mere escapist fairytales for kids have likely never read or watched much classic fantasy. Still, the genre is arguably at its best when darkness is not an end in itself but a backdrop for heroism and optimism to break through. In recent decades, these latter elements have seemingly been snuffed out by a growing fixation on gloom and darkness.

For example, despite all being influenced to some degree by *The Lord of the Rings*, the most popular fantasy television shows in recent memory—*Game of Thrones, The Witcher, The Wheel of Time, American Gods*, etc.—are largely anti-Tolkien in their approach.

Whereas the fantasy genre traditionally offered an escape from the grim and painful realities of life, now people must scamper back to reality to escape from these grim, violent, and hellish dystopian fantasy worlds.

Why is so much of today's imaginative storytelling fixated on darkness? Why have hopeful and optimistic narratives become out of fashion or reserved for children?

Too Grown Up for Optimism

Perhaps part of the reason for the trend toward darker storytelling is what we might dub *The Empire Strikes Back* hypothesis. Almost universally acknowledged as the "best" Star Wars film, *Empire* is also known as being the "dark" one (which is somewhat of a misnomer, as it is certainly *thematically* dark, but by no means *tonally* dark). Now, almost without exception, the two promises given to fans about upcoming sequels are that they will be "bigger" and "darker." Darker has become shorthand for "more mature." The implication is that dark and angsty themes are truer to real life, whereas bright and hopeful stories are comforting lies for sheltered children.

There is a certain degree of irony with this mindset. "Dark and gritty films are better because they more accurately reflect real life," declares the moviegoer in an air-conditioned home, watching a pristine 4K television, surrounded by more conveniences than the kings of the ancient world possessed. To indulge intentionally and repeatedly in dark and despairing stories is perhaps a luxury for a culture that often knows little of true misery or discomfort.

Of course, there is nothing inherently wrong with darker films. Many of the greatest films ever made have been dark and tragic. In fact, "tragedy" is arguably the oldest narrative genre. Storytelling *should* probe the darker nuances of the human experience. There is much pain and hurt in this life, and nobody makes it to the end of the journey without scars. Dark stories are powerful and necessary. They reflect a true and important part of the human experience—but *only* a part. To portray the full picture

of what it means to be human requires a healthy equilibrium of both darkness and light, a balance the gospel perfectly encapsulates.

The Gospel: Darkness & Light

The gospel is the greatest story ever told. No narrative has ever captured the fullness of life as accurately as the Bible does. Scripture holds nothing back in its raw exploration of both light and darkness. In the Bible, the sensual love poetry of *Song of Songs* exists alongside the dark, angsty psalms of David. The gospel story showcases the peak of human failure and despair while also laying the foundation for the unfathomable promise and hope of human redemption. The necessary co-existence of light and darkness in the gospel is evident in the stark contrast between the Cross and the Resurrection. The gospel is incomplete without both events.

In the same way, today's storytelling presents a false, or at least partial, understanding of human life without exploring the reality of both light and darkness. To indulge in unrelenting despair and darkness is like the Cross without the Resurrection. It tells the truth about pain and suffering but lies about the reality of eternal life and hope beyond that pain. On the other hand, to be immersed only in bright, cheerful narratives—as much Christian storytelling tends to do—is the Resurrection without the Cross. It offers feel-good sentiment and hope without telling the full truth about how much that joy cost.

That is not to suggest that all narratives must emphasize both elements. Not every story needs a redemptive arc. There are times when it is appropriate to dwell on the darkness of this world and to lament. Dark stories remind us that there is real evil in this world beyond the protective walls of our comfortable lives.

But Christians are ultimately called to live in the light **(1 John 1)**. Fantasy stories can be embraced in their full escapist glory, not as an escape from reality but an escape *to* a reality that seems far removed from present difficult circumstances. There is value in dark stories, but there is also power in hopeful tales that shine light into the darkness. There is no shame in mature adults enjoying a "happily ever after" story. Indeed, as the gospel beautifully reveals, perhaps no narrative comes closer to reality.

The Resurrection According to Hollywood

"Jesus said to her, 'I am the resurrection and the life. The one who believes in me, even if he dies, will live'" **(John 11:25)**.

Easter is coming. It's perhaps fitting that the celebration of a miraculous occurrence that took the entire world by surprise often arrives unexpectedly. Still, it is perplexing that the pivotal event in human history is often reduced to a blip on the calendar, appearing with little fanfare and departing quickly.

Consider the different ways the birth and resurrection of Jesus are celebrated. Christmas is not merely a day; it's a season. In the gospel—the "true myth" as C. S. Lewis put it—Christmas is a glorious moment, but the Resurrection of Jesus is the shocking plot twist, the climax, and the defining event. Why, then, is it so often overshadowed or downplayed? Part of the answer can be found in the stories we tell, the stories we don't tell, and perhaps the stories we *cannot* tell.

The Stories We Tell

A biographical movie about Charles Dickens is titled The Man Who Invented Christmas. Of course, Dickens did not invent the historical importance of Christmas, but he defined what might be called the "Christmas spirit." A Christmas Carol was revolutionary, arriving at a time when Christmas celebrations were falling out of favor. The reason the cherished yuletide story reflects so much of our contemporary understanding of Christmas is because it largely established the template. Stories about Christmas came to define the way people understood and celebrated the holiday.

Stories about Easter, on the other hand, are rare. We have "Christmas" movies, "Halloween" movies, and "summer" movies, but try to name three "Easter" movies. Nevertheless, the Easter story has influenced Hollywood, both directly and indirectly.

Resurrection Stories

Resurrection is a widespread motif in all mediums of storytelling. Mythologist Joseph Campbell introduced an influential theory called the "Monomyth" or "Hero's Journey," which argues that all stories are merely a re-telling—in part or in full— of the same universal story. One of the key stages in that archetypal story is the "resurrection" of the hero. We don't need to look far to find examples.

The Resurrection is the defining event of our human story, so it is unsurprising that it is often the pinnacle moment in the stories we tell.

From Harry Potter to Gandalf to Aslan to Neo to Obi-Wan Kenobi, countless self-sacrificial heroes have died and been resurrected. The resurrection theme is evident in more subtle ways as well, such as when heroes are not resurrected from literal death but are metaphorically reborn. Peter Parker in *Spider Man* (2002) is symbolically crucified with outstretched arms to stop a crashing train before rising again. Bruce Wayne in *The Dark Knight Rises* (2012) has his body broken and is imprisoned in a hellish pit before rising and returning as the savior of Gotham. An ad for AMC theaters that currently plays before every movie features Nicole Kidman describing the movie-going experience this way: "We're not just entertained, but somehow reborn."

I believe the prevelance of this theme is more than merely copying a familiar trope. Rather, there is something within humanity that is wired to make sense of the world through narratives of resurrection and rebirth. The Resurrection is the defining event of our human story, so it is unsurprising that it is often the pinnacle moment in the stories we tell.

The Passion of the Christ

Occasionally, the literal Resurrection of Jesus becomes the focus of a movie. The most famous example is Mel Gibson's *Passion of the Christ* (2014). The film is a prime example of the difficulty in cinematically depicting the event. It focuses primarily on the physical violence, which made it the highest grossing R-rated movie in history and compelled many Christians to break their long-standing "no R-rated movies" rule!

The emphasis on violence reflects and reinforces a prevalent mindset. Every Easter, the Crucifixion is described in almost hyperbolic terms. Preachers often stress that crucifixion was the worst, most painful death imaginable and that Jesus suffered more than anyone ever has on our behalf. At times, the presentation amounts to a spiritual guilt trip, as we are shown bruised and bloody images of Jesus and told that we are ultimately responsible.

Christians should be reminded of the seriousness of our sin and what it cost to redeem us. But, in a way, emphasizing Jesus' physical suffering actually diminishes what he accomplished through the Cross and the Empty Tomb. What Jesus suffered physically was excruciating, but he was crucified beside two criminals who experienced the same agonizing fate. According to legend, Peter was crucified upside-down, going one step further than his Lord. Christian martyrs have been burned, skinned alive, fed to lions, and impaled. In fact, many Christians throughout history have arguably suffered more physically painful deaths than Jesus did.

The true power of Jesus' suffering is the spiritual impact it had: "God made him who had no sin to be sin for us, so that in him we might become the righteousness of

In a way, emphasizing Jesus' physical suffering actually diminishes what he accomplished through the Cross and the Empty Tomb.

God" **(2 Corinthians 5:21)**. That unfathomable reality defies cinematic visualization. How can a movie show Christ's anguish of taking the sin of the world onto his shoulders? It can't, which is why directors like Mel Gibson have settled for an overwhelmingly earthly and physical crucifixion story. It also explains why crucifixion movies are far more common than resurrection films.

The Greatest Eucatastrophe

Movies and stories can reflect the Resurrection, but like Moses hiding his face from the glory of God, they offer only a small flicker of the awesome, overwhelming power of that monumental event. The fingerprints of the Easter story are all over Hollywood—directly or indirectly—but something is inevitably missing. Movies can be helpful reminders of Christ's sacrifice and victory, but the Resurrection is far more glorious than any movie can show.

J. R. R. Tolkien, author of *The Lord of the Rings*, coined the delightful term, "Eucatastrophe." The word means the sudden, unexpected reversal of fate. A "happy ending," but in the most profound sense

Movies and stories can reflect the Resurrection, but like Moses hiding his face from the glory of God, they offer only a small flicker of the awesome, overwhelming power of that monumental event.

possible. Tolkien believed that this was the most important task of all fairy stories, and that Easter is the perfect example. As we prepare our hearts to celebrate Easter, I am reminded of one of my favorite descriptions of the Resurrection:

"And I concluded by saying that the Resurrection was the greatest 'eucatastrophe' possible in the greatest Fairy Story – and produces that essential emotion: Christian joy which produces tears because it is qualitatively so like sorrow, because it comes from those places where Joy and Sorrow are at one, reconciled, as selfishness and altruism are lost in Love." – Tolkien

The Gospel According to Disaster Movies

There are three certainties in life: death, taxes, and at least one silly disaster flick hitting theaters in the early part of the year. I will admit that I have a soft spot for the genre, even though it lacks the cinematic elements I normally enjoy—nuanced characters, a thought-provoking story—and leans hard into the elements I typically detest—mindless CGI spectacle and over-the-top action. Much like a car crash, there's something about a disaster that makes it hard to look away.

No one watches a disaster movie expecting high cinema or to wrestle with deep philosophical themes. They want to see stuff blow up and get destroyed. Perhaps more than any other movie genre, disaster films are driven by spectacle. Nevertheless, I believe the genre actually has some value for Christian viewers beyond mindless entertainment. Here are four ways disaster movies can provide beneficial viewing.

1. Humility & Perspective

Like the architects of the tower of Babel, today's society takes great pride in its own achievement. We have declared ourselves the most technologically advanced and enlightened people ever to walk the planet—but none of that matters when the moon suddenly comes hurtling toward earth.

While the plots are exaggerated fiction, there is something sobering about watching how futile people truly are against the overwhelming powers of nature. For an arrogant culture that prides itself on being in control of its own destiny, disaster films reorient our perspective and inspire humility before the power of God and his creation.

2. Human Nature Exposed During Times of Crisis

A central theme in many disaster movies is the human response to a crisis. Spectacle is important, but a two-hour runtime of uninterrupted disaster scenes would quickly become tiresome. Whether a disaster flick is engaging (or uninteresting) depends on its characters. The disastrous circumstances set the stage to probe human nature.

Just like real-life tragedies, fictionalized tragedy brings out the best and worst of human nature. Some characters inevitably rise to the occasion and heroically sacrifice themselves for the greater good. Other characters use the tragedy as an opportunity to exploit other people's misfortune or indulge in carnal passions. Disaster movies may not always be the most profound character studies, but part of the experience of watching these films is to ask the question, "What would I do in this scenario?" (Spoiler alert: I would be dead. Very quickly. Sorry, and good luck!).

3. Value of Human Life

At first glance, this theme may seem ironic or even absurd. Most disaster movies feature a staggering amount of death and devastation, which is implied if not always shown. Admittedly, some disaster films glorify death and turn the loss of human life into an entertaining spectacle. Much time and energy is spent in Hollywood writers' rooms brainstorming new and innovative ways for characters to meet their untimely ends. Christians should be cautious about celebrating death, even in the realm of fiction.

On the other hand, disaster movies can underscore the value of life. The sanctity of human life is rarely understood as clearly as when it is viewed against the backdrop of widespread death and loss following a real-world disaster. Legitimate arguments can be made that constant exposure to cinematic violence has desensitized viewers. But disaster movies can evoke the same reaction to tragic loss as real-world tragedies, without the real-world consequences. Fictionalized tragedy may provoke an emotional response of a far lesser degree, but that does not render it valueless. The best disaster films compel audiences to root for characters to persevere against the odds, a struggle made all the more praiseworthy by the torrent of death and devastation around them.

4. God's Perfectly Balanced Creation

Few disaster movies put God front and center, unless the infamous "End Times" Christian films are counted among their number. Yet, few genres focus more directly on God's creation than disaster films do. For many disaster films, the inciting incident involves some disruption of the created order. In the recent disaster movie *Moonfall*, a character spouts dialogue about how finely tuned and perfectly balanced the moon's orbit is and that knocking it even a small degree off its course would lead to utter annihilation of earth and extinction of humanity. Christian philosophers and apologists have been making similar arguments for centuries! By demonstrating the devastation and horror that results from an unbalanced universe, disaster films implicitly point to the glorious perfection of God's creation.

The Gospel According to Time-Travel Movies

The possibility of time travel has captivated people for a long time. Ever since science-fiction master H. G. Wells popularized the concept with his 1895 novel *The Time Machine*, storytellers have been further exploring the genre. Time-travel narratives remain as popular today as ever. The latest time-travel movie, *The Adam Project*, is currently the #1 film on Netflix, following in the wake of other recent films like *Tenet, The Tomorrow War,* and *Avengers: Endgame*. There is something about travel stories that continues to intrigue and engage audiences.

Recently, I took a similar approach to another popular movie genre in *The Gospel According to Disaster Movies*. I did not plan for that article to launch a series or receive any follow-up. Yet, as I've thought about the time-travel genre—another personal favorite—I've realized several ways that these movies can challenge Christian viewers. No, these Hollywood films are not gospel presentations with an altar call instead of end credits, but below are three ways the time-travel genre echoes the gospel.

In Time & Out of Time

There is no reality as unavoidable or fundamental to the human experience as time. We are quite literally under the influence of time *all the time*. The same might be said of forces like gravity, yet airplanes exist. Technology and brainiac science allow us to manipulate and transcend even gravity. The simple act of jumping represents a small and transitory triumph over gravity. There is no such victory over time (no, daylight savings doesn't count!).

The inescapable reality of time is perhaps why fictional time-travel stories are such a fun playground to explore. What if we moved backward through time? What would happen to us if we went back in time and killed our ancestors, as in the famous "grandfather paradox" thought experiment?

What unintended consequences would there be in the present if we altered the past in subtle ways?

Time is fundamental to our lives, but there is a reality outside of time. God is not bound to time **(2 Peter 3:8)**. God existed in the beginning **(Genesis 1:1, John 1:1)**. Notably, even this biblical language reflects the limitation of human understanding. God existed in the beginning, but *what is our* beginning? As an eternal being, God has no beginning. The "beginning" in these verses refers to our beginning—the beginning of time itself.

While time travel will likely remain exclusive to the realm of imaginative science fiction, the Bible reveals that one day we *will* escape time. Christians experience time while on earth—the good and the bad— but we are ultimately destined for eternity **(John 3:16)**.

Past, Present, and Future

Time travel can go in two directions—backward or forward. Whether returning to the past or transporting into the distant future, a central theme in many time-travel stories is the inseparable relationship between the past, present, and future. This idea is evident in movie titles such as *Back to the Future* or *X-Men: Days of Future Past*. It is perhaps most famously depicted by the three ghosts of Charles Dickens' *A Christmas Carol*. Time travel allows characters to move between different points in time, but the moral quandaries and narrative tension is predicated on an understanding that decisions and actions can have a far-reaching impact, sending ripples throughout time.

The crucial relationship between past, present, and future is consistent with the gospel. Christianity is both a backward-looking and forward-looking faith. The gospel requires Christians to look back to the original sin in Eden and to the Crucifixion and Resurrection, historic events some 2000 years in the past. At the same time, Christians also look longingly ahead to the second coming of Jesus and the glorious new creation **(Revelation 21)**. Paul captures this beautiful union of past and future when he writes, "Being confident of this, that he who began a good work in you will carry it on to completion until the day of Christ Jesus" **(Philippians 1:6)**.

The Importance of Now

Despite being a genre about journeying into the past or future, the most interesting time-travel stories are always fundamentally about the *now*. At its best, the imaginative ability to travel outside of time provides enlightening perspective and commentary on the present. Traveling to the past allows characters (and, by extension, audiences) to explore the decisions and events that led to present-day circumstances. In a similar way, journeying into the future is a prophetic—and often sobering—forecast about what consequences await humanity if we do not make the necessary adjustments ("Artificial Intelligence is a really bad idea, guys. Trust me!" — Every Time Traveler From The Future).

As already noted, Christianity is both a forward and backward-looking faith. Nevertheless, every Christian's divine calling is to the present. Jesus commissioned his disciples to be salt and light in the time in which they live. In many time-travel stories, there is a reverberation of the biblical wisdom, "There is a time for everything, and a season for every activity under the heavens" **(Ecclesiastes 3:1)**. Time is a part of God's perfect design for his creation. Past, present, and future all matter, but they must be kept in their proper place. As humans, we do not gain mastery over time by breaking out of it or manipulating it but by embracing it as God intended.

This idea is captured in the famous question put to Queen Esther: "And who knows but that you have come to your royal position for such a time as this?" **(Esther 4:14)**. The past prepares us, and our actions will have future consequences for good or evil, but what matters most is what we do in the present. Time is a fun concept to explore, but ultimately Christians are called to live faithfully in such a time as this.

Batman v. Christianity: Reflections on a Complicated Hero

"The most important thing in life is always to be yourself. Unless you can be Batman, in which case, always be Batman."

Everyone loves Batman. Since debuting in *Detective Comics* on March 30, 1939, Batman has appeared in more than twenty feature films, more than a dozen television shows, countless comic books and graphic novels, and become a global pop culture icon. Some people have suggested that superheroes have become the mythology of our time. Far from mere children's stories about people in capes and tights, superheroes provide archetypal narratives, teach moral lessons, and wrestle with deep philosophical worldview issues (and they do it all while rocking spandex).

A common mistake Christians make regarding fictional stories and characters is the expectation that the heroes must conform to our own Christian values. Thus, when Christians make movies or write books, the protagonist is typically a Christian. Batman is captivating because he is *not* a typical hero. We appreciate and admire Batman, but we dare not imitate him. Unlike Superman or Wonder Woman, he does not provide virtuous ideals to which we should aspire. The value of the Batman character is that he says the quiet part out loud. He makes us uncomfortable by exposing the darker aspects of our own human nature and probing the gray area between holiness and human depravity.

Below are four ways Christians can glean insight and wisdom from Batman movies.

Justice v. Vengeance

Eighty-three years (and counting) of Batman stories provides an interesting case study for how society views superheroes. Much has changed since *Batman: The Movie* (1966), when Adam West's goofy Batman battled a rubber shark with a

The Bible calls Christians to fight for justice and shine light into the darkness, but it also affirms that vengeance belongs to God alone.

can of Anti-Shark Bat Repellent. Christopher Nolan's critically acclaimed *Dark Knight trilogy* (2005-2012) and Matt Reeves' *The Batman* (2022) have plunged further into the dark abyss of the Caped Crusader's complicated persona. When asked his identity in *The Batman*, the masked vigilante (played by Robert Pattinson) simply growls, "I'm vengeance."

An engrossing theme in these recent Batman movies is the tension between justice and vengeance. Batman is both a member of the honorable Justice League and a violent manifestation of vengeance

in Gotham. This tension is evident in scripture as well. The Bible calls Christians to fight for justice and shine light into the darkness, but it also affirms that vengeance belongs to God alone **(Romans 12:19)**.

The words from the classic novel *The Count of Monte Cristo*, a precursor to the Batman stories, come to mind: "He decided it was human hatred and not divine vengeance that had plunged him into this abyss," and "[h]e felt he had passed beyond the bounds of vengeance, and that he could no longer say, 'God is for and with me.'" What are the limits of earthly justice? When do we go too far and infringe upon that which belongs to God alone? Batman doesn't provide easy answers, but he is willing to grapple with these difficult questions.

Human v. Divine

Batman will forever be linked to Superman. The Mount Rushmore of superheroes begins with those two. The famed heroes offer a fascinating juxtaposition. Superman is a traditional "Christ-figure" archetype as a quasi-divine being who comes to earth as its protector and self-sacrificial savior. It is perhaps a reflection of an increasingly secularized society that Superman has been largely left behind. In the last 35 years, there have been ten Batman-centric films compared to Superman's two. Christopher Nolan, producer of the most recent Superman film, *Man of Steel* (2013), said, "He has the most extraordinary ideals to live up to. He's very God-like in a lot of ways and it's been difficult to imagine that in a contemporary setting."

In stark contrast, Batman has never been more relatable or popular. Batman is a hero—sometimes an anti-hero—but never

a savior. He is not a divine outsider who has come to earth to rescue it, but rather a visceral, flawed, and fundamentally human response to evil and injustice. Films like *Wonder Woman* (2017) show that there is still an appetite for optimistic heroes and benevolent saviors, but the balance has clearly shifted. It is fitting that in Zach Snyder's *Batman v. Superman* (2016), Batman is the surprising victor, a reflection of a culture that has increasingly abandoned faith in the divine and placed its hopes for salvation in human might, power, and rage.

Superhero v. Civilian Duty

Despite what every marketing campaign promises, most recent versions of Batman are remarkably similar. There are nuanced differences, but once the mask is on and he starts pounding goons, there's only so much room for variation. What truly differentiates the Batman stories is Bruce Wayne. In a film like The *Dark Knight Rises* (2012), for example, Batman is in the suit and cape for only 13% of the screen time. How a movie depicts Bruce Wayne is arguably more essential than how it does Batman.

The "alter ego" is a standard trope in most superhero stories. Typically, the purpose is to blend in or hide from the world, driven by an understandable selfishness and the desire to balance superhero responsibilities with a relatively normal life. In the best Batman

> It is perhaps a reflection of an increasingly secularized society that Superman has been largely left behind.

stories, however, Bruce Wayne breaks from this mindset. There is a foundational unity and partnership between Bruce Wayne and the Batman persona.

Part of what makes the unity of Batman and Bruce Wayne unique is that, unlike many of his super-powered friends, Batman is a powerless mortal. When asked what his superpower is, Ben Affleck's Bruce Wayne humorously says, "I'm rich." While many superhero stories showcase the limitations of the average citizen and the need for special heroes, Batman explores the limitations of the superhero persona and the need for normal citizens to join the fight against injustice. This idea is captured in Commissioner Gordan's famous lines at the end of *The Dark Knight* (2008): "He's the hero Gotham deserves, but not the one it needs right now."

Sin v. The New Creation

Gotham City is almost as much a character in the drama as Batman himself. Beyond the undeniably cool aesthetic, Gotham is also a magnifying glass that exposes the worst aspects of human society and the depths of human depravity. Batman never succeeds in cleaning up Gotham. His efforts are a drop in the ocean of the corruption and sin that infests the city. A Batman story rarely ends on an optimistic note. Far from achieving victory, the stories declare the futility of even humanity's best efforts to overcome its sinful, fallen nature. God is perceivable in Gotham largely through his silence, painting a bleak picture of a world—or at least a city—without God. The absence of the divine in Gotham City provides Christians with a raw picture of sin and a renewed hopefulness for the coming of the new creation **(Revelation 21-22)**.

The Disappearance of Superman & Idealism

What in the world happened to Superman?

If something flies across your TV screen these days, it's likely a bird or a plane, because it certainly isn't Superman. In an era when superhero films are more prevalent than ever before, it's perplexing that the world's most famous superhero is nowhere to be seen.

While the current "in-crowd" of popular superheroes is obviously not among the chief concerns for Christians today, the curious disappearance of Superman may provide insight into our culture and into ourselves.

The Disappearance of Superman

Countless lesser-known and increasingly bizarre comic-book characters have flooded theaters in recent years, but the Man of Steel remains largely relegated to the sidelines. Meanwhile, his angsty and brooding Justice League colleague Batman is rarely out of the cultural spotlight.

Consider this: *Superman IV: The Quest for Peace* (the final Christopher Reeve movie) hit theaters a few months after I was born. Since then, there have been only two Superman films— *Superman Returns* (2006) and *Man of Steel* (2013). In that same time, Batman has starred in eight or nine films (even more if you count *The Lego Batman Movie* or other animated features). I watched the last Superman movie in a theater as part of my brother's bachelor party. He's now married with four kids. It's been a while.

The character has appeared in several ensemble films, including *Batman v. Superman* (2016) and *Justice League...* twice (2017, 2021). But these movies feel more like an attempt to buoy the superhero with more popular characters. Even the recent animated film *DC League of Super-Pets* (a story about Superman's dog) is a surprising box-office failure. He may be invulnerable, but Supes can't seem to catch a break.

The Disappearance of Idealism

The most recent Henry Cavill iteration of Superman has a slightly darker, grittier edge than earlier versions (and he finally got the memo not to wear his underwear on the outside), but the character has remained essentially the same over the years. He may not have changed much, but culture certainly has.

Christopher Nolan, producer of Superman's most recent film, *Man of Steel* (2013), perhaps said it best: "He has the most extraordinary ideals to live up to. He's very God-like in a lot of ways and it's been difficult to imagine that in a contemporary setting."

Before concluding that today's world is simply too dark to make space for such an idealistic hero, we should remember that the original Superman comic debuted shortly before World War II. Things were grim then too. In fact, much of the initial appeal of the character was undoubtedly due to the difficult real-world circumstances. Superman was a beacon of goodness in a world that was losing

its grip on it. These days, however, many audiences seem to want their heroes to reflect harsh reality rather than transcend it.

Earnestness has become associated with childish escapism. Today's storytellers seem almost abashed to depict characters who strive for goodness and truth. The superheroes who aren't dark and gritty anti-heroes are typically portrayed as goofy or tongue-in-cheek. For example, in the most recent MCU film *Thor: Love and Thunder*, Thor is anything but "dark." He is also a bumbling buffoon. The implication is obvious: "It's just silly entertainment, but everyone knows the *real* world isn't bright and optimistic like that!" As society drifts further away from hope and belief in God, it makes sense that divine, god-like heroes suddenly feel outdated.

Striving Toward an Ideal

The current fixation on deeply flawed heroes may stem from the wider conversation on identity and our longing for affirmation. Flawed, imperfect anti-heroes affirm us. They suggest that "heroes look just like you." They have anger problems, act selfishly, and battle against themselves as much as against their enemies. Heroes like Superman, on the other hand, make us feel inadequate or powerless. They're too good to be true, so why bother?

But the power of an ideal is not in achieving the end goal but in constantly striving for it. It is about the journey as much as the destination. This concept is biblical. In the Sermon on the Mount, Jesus declared, "Be perfect, therefore, as your heavenly Father is perfect" **(Matthew 5:48)**. Perfection is a lofty, unachievable ideal. The remark comes right after Christ paints an idealistic picture for his followers to love their enemies. Christians have struggled to live up to that teaching ever since, but it remains a worthy goal.

Paul took on the responsibility of setting the example for the church at Corinth: "You are to imitate me, just as I imitate Christ" **(1 Corinthians 11:1)**. The Corinthians were ultimately called to reflect Christ, not Paul. But the apostle provided a tangible (if imperfect) example for them to follow.

There is power in ideals, in gazing high and striving toward lofty ends. Ideals don't imply childish naivety about the harsh realities in the world; they are motivators to overcome those realities, even just a little.

In fact, all superheroes—even the dark, gritty ones—represent ideals. The challenge of all superhero stories is to inspire ordinary people through characters who are anything but ordinary. They are, by definition, not just heroes. They are *super*heroes.

There's certainly a place for flawed, relatable anti-heroes. Many of the best comic-book stories ever told have showcased such characters. There are valuable lessons to be learned by watching characters struggle against their flawed nature.

There is also a need for idealistic heroes, for characters who remind us of the goodness and truth that are difficult to see in our present circumstances. Some heroes enable us to make sense of our dark world; others help us remember that there is more to life than the darkness around us. Superman has spent a lot of time watching from the sidelines, but it feels as though there is a quiet rumbling in our culture for his inevitable return. Superman is a symbol and a powerful reminder that goodness wins. Christians can be encouraged by the knowledge that this divine ideal is not, in fact, too good to be true.

How Much Entertainment is Too much Entertainment?

We've all been there. We're sitting in our favorite restaurant, lethargic, full, and feeling the first pangs of an inevitable stomachache, but there's still some delicious food in front of us. We take "just one more bite." Then another. And another. After all, we've paid hard-earned money for it. So we keep chewing long after the food brings any semblance of delight. This imagery keeps coming to mind as I think about the current state of entertainment. How much entertainment is too much?

It's not hyperbolic to suggest that there is currently more easily accessible, high-quality entertainment available than at any point in human history. Yet there is also an increased dissatisfaction, weariness, and ambivalence toward it. While the mere idea of a new release might once have brought uncontained glee ("Star Wars on TV?!?" or "A Marvel show that directly connects with the larger MCU?!?"), the actualization of it has left many people feeling oddly numb and indifferent ("Maybe a Boba Fett show was a bad idea after all," or "Yet another Marvel series? Hope it's better than the last one.")

Perhaps it's more anecdotal than scientific, but as someone engaged in the pop culture conversation, I've encountered the sentiment more often in recent days. Data suggests that audiences are still watching these shows in mass numbers, but the surrounding discourse reveals that enthusiasm is in short supply.

Too Much of a Good Thing

There are many reasons why the abundant entertainment options fail to excite as expected. One factor may simply be that entertainment, like seemingly everything else in our culture, has been sucked into the all-consuming maw of contemporary politics. Thus, engaging with today's entertainment can feel like a chore, an extension of our current problems rather than an escape from them.

At the same time, there may also be a simpler explanation. We have become disillusioned with today's entertainment because we have far too much of it. We're drowning in the deluge of options. Streaming platforms like Netflix now boast such sprawling media libraries that they've implemented an algorithm to choose on our behalf.

Even our terminology reflects our shifting mindset toward entertainment. Movies and television shows, once deemed an innovative artform, have now been reduced to "content." Streaming companies promise subscribers more options than ever before, with the emphasis placed on the quantity. Studios and streaming platforms compete in an arms race to churn out more and more content to feed the machine of consumerism. A show like *The Rings of Power* or *Obi-Wan Kenobi* should feel like big cultural landmark events. Instead, they seem like just the latest batch of content to come off the assembly line.

The existence of "lots of stuff" obviously doesn't necessitate that people must watch it. No one forces me to shove another bite of Thanksgiving turkey into my already stuffed belly either. There is something about the abundant availability of a good thing that provokes overindulgence. The "more is more" mentality of constant content fosters a culture of consumerism. It's not unusual for someone to share, "I'm finally catching up on _____," in reference to an episode that aired only a few days ago or to trudge dutifully through a lackluster Marvel show so they don't get left behind in the larger narrative.

Moderation and Discernment

When it comes to Christianity and entertainment, the discussion typically focuses on how to navigate the endless jungle of today's entertainment choices. Implicit in this mindset is a general acceptance that Christians are unavoidably enmeshed in that jungle. We question *what* to watch but rarely *if* we should. In fact, it is because most Christians are deeply immersed in entertainment that the questions of how to navigate it have become so relevant.

The Bible is largely silent regarding entertainment. It provides several general principles, but no specific rules. The lack of clear instructions regarding entertainment may suggest that entertainment was not a primary issue. Establishing foundational theological doctrine and church policy was more important.

Another reason the early church didn't focus much on entertainment is likely because leisure occupied a small portion of people's lives. The theater and poetry were popular, but first-century citizens weren't vegging on the couch for hours every evening. The average American spends more time engaged with entertainment on a weekend than first-century citizens may have experienced in a month.

That is not to suggest that enjoying entertainment is inherently bad. The first-century lifestyle is by no means the platonic ideal. There is nothing wrong with relaxing and being entertained after a long day. Recreation is healthy, and stories can be a powerful means of understanding ourselves and our world. The danger is not in the activity but in overindulgence.

How much entertainment is too much entertainment? There is no one-size-fits-all answer, as much as Christians might wish there was. The Bible doesn't give specific restrictions or establish a quantifiable threshold. Each Christian must exhibit discernment and moderation in this area. A persistent theme throughout Proverbs is the importance of prudence and self-control. Paul used the vivid metaphor of athletes' strict training **(1 Corinthians 9:24-27)**. Athletes need to rest and know their physical and mental limits. But those moments of rest are to recharge them for the more important activity ahead.

Entertainment can be good and healthy in moderation. But when we begin to feel weary or drained by it, we must ask ourselves if we've crossed the line into overindulgence.

Expanding Eden: Christians as Cultivators of Culture

The human story begins in a garden.

Despite what many now believe, the garden was not just another chance stop on homo sapiens' aimless evolutionary journey from primordial soup to the skyscrapers of New York City. The truth is far more astonishing than that. Humans were *created* for the garden. The Bible reveals, "Now the Lord God had planted a garden in the east, in Eden; and there he put the man he had formed" **(Genesis 2:8)**. The garden was planted and set aside by God to be the first dwelling for his prized creation.

Eden has become synonymous with a utopian paradise. We imagine that had Adam and Eve resisted the forbidden fruit, we still might be enjoying the cool shade of the garden to this day. Yet, even before the Fall, God gave humans a mandate: "Be fruitful and increase in number; fill the earth and subdue it. Rule over the fish in the sea and the birds in the sky and over every living creature that moves on the ground" **(Genesis 1:28)**. Filling and subduing the earth cannot be accomplished from a garden. Adam and Eve were placed in the garden, but it was not intended to be a forever home.

So, why a garden? Scripture provides the answer: "The Lord God took the man and put him in the Garden of Eden to work it and take care of it" **(Genesis 2:15)**. The Garden of Eden appears to have been intended as a sort of training ground. In the garden, humans would learn how to care for God's creation and become creators themselves. Just as God first named his creations and then invited Adam to join the creative act by naming the animals **(Genesis 2:20)**, God also planted the garden in Eden and then invited humans to go forth and cultivate the earth. From the beginning of our story, we were created to be cultivators of creation.

A Creative Mandate

Exile from Eden does not absolve humans from the mandate to cultivate the earth. Christians need not yearn for a return to a place that was only intended as a training ground. Rather, we should recall the lessons God intended for us to learn in the garden and then apply them to the world around us today.

There is a nostalgic longing for the simplicity of Eden. As some preachers have declared, "Cities only come after the Fall!" Yet, there is also a unique beauty in cities. Metropolitan areas have always been hubs for art and culture, for innovation and discovery. A world filled with only gardeners and farmers is likely a world without Beethoven, Michelangelo, or Shakespeare; without airplanes and space exploration. It is a world where significantly fewer people have had the opportunity to hear the gospel proclaimed. The first disciples may have been chosen from rural communities, but the first churches began in the cities.

Christians cannot return to Eden, but we can cultivate the world around us to be more like that beautiful garden sanctuary.

> Christians cannot return to Eden, but we can cultivate the world around us to be more like that beautiful garden sanctuary.

Christian Cultivators

Christians can be many things in relation to culture. Critical. Antagonistic. Fearful. Enslaved. But how often is the church seen as a cultivator of culture? Are Christians tilling the cultural soil, plucking the ugly weeds, and planting new trees to grow, flourish, and produce fruit? Christians should infuse art, beauty, and meaningful storytelling into any community where God places us. A church steeple should be a signpost pointing hurt and broken people to where they can find Edenic peace and sanctuary.

The world desperately needs faithful Christians to fulfill our creative mandate. The enduring allure of Eden is fostered by a modern world that looks nothing like a garden. Today's culture is more akin to an assembly-line factory or a bitter war zone than a peaceful garden where people can walk with God in the cool of the day.

Unfortunately, Christians do not always live up to this wonderful calling. We often desire our own private Edens but have little care to fulfill our creative mandate in the world beyond our protective garden walls. But Christians are not called to hide from or bemoan culture. We are commissioned to cultivate it into something beautiful.

The Religiosity of Fandom

Pop culture is dominated by fandoms. For better or worse, the entertainment industry caters to the expansive communities that unite around popular franchises or intellectual properties, from Marvel to Star Wars to Disney and beyond.

Christians tend to attribute "religion" to almost everything. Thus, atheism becomes a religion, the shopping mall becomes a sacred site, and entertainment fandoms become religious communities. This mindset, while not wholly off base, is a bit too cute. When everything is a religion, religion is cheapened. If religion is a fundamental orientation or framework for understanding the world, then being a superfan of a particular comic-book franchise, for example, is something different. Further, many religious people are also a part of one or more of these fandoms.

While it may be an overstatement to label fandoms "religions" in any meaningful sense, the current allure of fandoms certainly reflects religious elements. As society drifts away from religion, it's perhaps unsurprising that many religious tendencies have manifested themselves in other areas, such as pop-culture fandoms. In a sense, fandoms serve as a mirror reflecting both the best and worst of our religious tendencies.

The Need for Community

God declared, "It is not good for man to be alone" **(Genesis 2:18)**. There is a deep human longing for community. In this digital age when social isolation is more convenient than ever and technology has chewed away at many traditional social gathering places (such as shopping centers and movie theaters), our need for community is as strong as ever.

One example of our desire for community is evident in the current debate about the "binging" model of TV streaming versus the old-fashioned staggered-release framework. At the onset of streaming, binging was a viewer's paradise. The idea of gorging oneself on hours of on-demand viewing without commercials seemed almost too good to be true. Several years later, the realization has set in that part of what makes shows enjoyable is the communal experience of watching them and the subsequent discussions that happen every week around the digital water cooler. In other words, the communal experience and interaction of fandom.

There's a prevalent belief that the younger generations are staunchly individualistic and that technology fosters an isolated existence. While that view contains some truth, many young adults use technology to connect with communities and fandoms. There is a reason for the immense popularity of YouTube "reaction" videos, in which viewers watch someone else watch a new movie trailer or video. Society has a deep desire to share communal experiences in a digital world.

The younger generations are flocking away from the church en masse, leading some Christians to have a cynical attitude toward fandoms ("If only these kids would be as excited about worshiping God as they are about watching superheroes in spandex..."). Yet, the popularity of these massive fandoms is a positive sign. It indicates that the digital world has not—*cannot*—erase our God-created need for fellowship and community, a need the church can satisfy.

The Need for Unity

The appeal of fandoms is not just that they provide community in the sense of large masses of people. It's more specifically about the yearning for a *unified* community. The allure of events like Comic-Con or Star Wars Celebration is that a diverse community has a shared affection for something. Representation in its best, non-propagandistic form is driven by this desire for fandoms to be a place where everyone can find belonging.

Unification is another longing Christianity satisfies. The Apostle Paul wrote, "There is neither Jew nor Gentile, neither slave nor free, nor is there male and female, for you are all one in Christ Jesus" **(Galatians 3:28)**. When the Christian movement exploded in the first century, it was initially driven largely by those on the fringes of society (women, slaves, the poor, etc.). The gospel was the great unifier. It's *still* the great unifier. The church should reflect the idealistic dream of fandoms, in which every type and variety of person is united in Christ.

Need for Order and Control

Fandoms often reflect the better aspects of religion. Unfortunately, they frequently exemplify the worst as well. It rarely takes long for a large community to establish a rigid, legalistic orthodoxy. In fandom, this tendency leads to ridiculous conversations like, "Real fans know that..." or crusades against the heresy of Amazon's Lord of the Rings ("You seriously claim to be a fan of *Lord of the Rings*, but you don't even know the difference between the Ainulinadalë and the Akallabêth? SMH"). Buzz words like "gatekeeping" or "toxic" are now frequently volleyed around within fandom.

The worst of fandoms inevitably devolve into the worst of religion because they are driven by the same selfish, sinful tendency: a holier-than-thou pharisaical pride that elevates us at the expense of others. It's unfortunate when pop-culture fandoms are polluted by these flaws, but it's far more tragic when the church is. The Christian community is called to be better: "Now may the God who gives endurance and encouragement grant you harmony with one another in Christ Jesus, so that with one mind and one voice you may glorify the God and Father of our Lord Jesus Christ" **(Romans 15:5-6)**. As many pop-culture fandoms become increasingly toxic, may the church be a welcoming and united community where diversity is united under the banner of Christ.

Should Christians Separate the Art from the Artist?

Can Christians enjoy good art made by unbelievers or people of depraved moral character?

The question of separating the art from the artist is not unique to the church. Mainstream culture is grappling with this issue, as demonstrated by the upcoming *We Need to Talk About Cosby* documentary, the messy fall from grace of pop-culture cult hero Joss Whedon, and the many fans now trying to divorce their beloved *Harry Potter* franchise from J. K. Rowling. The predicament is amplified with social media providing greater access to artists. For better or worse, people today know more about the daily thoughts and actions of creators than ever before.

The question is relevant across the cultural spectrum but is perhaps thornier for Christians. As a people set apart and called to a higher moral standard, Christians can feel uneasy about enjoying art and entertainment created by people who do not share or are antagonistic toward their religious faith.

Despite these valid concerns, Christians can—and *should*—separate the art from the artist.

Good Art by Bad People

The reluctance to separate the art from the artists has prevented many Christians from enjoying excellent works of art. To limit permissible art to that made by Christians or to creators who pass a certain threshold of virtue is to erase many of the greatest books, musical compositions, paintings, and films ever created.

Scripture clearly establishes that the ability to create works of artistic excellence and beauty is not restricted to the faithful. *All* people are created in the image of God, so it is unsurprising that unbelievers stumble upon truth and goodness through the arts, just as they have in the sciences and every other arena of human experience.

When describing what Christians should fixate on Paul wrote, "Finally, brothers and sisters, whatever is true, whatever is noble, whatever is right, whatever is pure, whatever is lovely, whatever is admirable—if anything is excellent or praiseworthy—think about such things" **(Philippians 4:8)**.

Christians should affirm the good, the true, and the beautiful whenever and wherever we find it—even when it is produced by the hands of disagreeable people.

If an opinion about the artistic quality of a work drastically changes due to a new insight about the artist's character or worldview, then the opinion was never based on artistic quality. A moral judgment of the artist and an aesthetic judgment of the art should remain distinct. In fact, even a moral judgment of *the art* should be kept separate from any aesthetic considerations. For example, Christians can affirm the technical excellence of a song while strongly condemning the vulgarity or distorted worldview the lyrics express.

Bad Art by Good People

Separating the art from the artist is typically considered in the context of good art made by "bad" people. But the reverse is also true. If "bad" people can make good art, then "good" people can make bad art. Are Christians duty-bound to affirm and praise shabby art if the artist is a lovely, God-fearing believer?

Unfortunately, the church can often be poor or shallow judges of art. Many Christians celebrate the agreeable rather than the excellent. They lavish praise on a faith-based film about the power of prayer or the sanctity of life not because the film is artistically commendable but simply because they agree with the theology or morality it espouses.

Unfortunately, the church can often be poor or shallow judges of art. Many Christians celebrate the agreeable rather than the excellent.

A simple test is to swap the artist's Christian faith for any alternative religion. If the art mentions God, imagine that it is referring to a deity other than the biblical God. Now evaluate the work of art. Is that popular song on Christian radio still artistically excellent? Can we acknowledge that despite not agreeing with the message or lifestyle of the musician, the lyrics are poetic and the music is technically superb?

Why does it matter? What harm is there in celebrating art made by fellow believers, even if the art is of poor quality?

Christians *should* support Christian artists. At the same time, praising art based on the artist's character alone sets a low artistic bar and provides little incentive to surpass it. Thoughtlessly affirming any bad work of art created by good people fosters a culture of good people making bad art.

In the Bible, whenever artistry is described, there is always an emphasis on the work being "skillfully done" **(Ex. 31; 1 Chron. 28; 2 Chron. 2:13)**. God is glorified through artistic excellence, and art made for his glory ought to represent him well. There is a reason why praise bands spend time practicing key changes and vocal harmonies rather than devoting the entire practice to Bible study and developing their characters. Character matters, but so does artistic excellence. Separating the art from the artist allows the church to affirm godly character, while also cultivating a standard of artistic excellence.

A Universal Language

Artistic excellence should be a universal language, a common ground for people of all religious faiths and worldviews. There are plenty of valid reasons for a Christian to avoid art created by non-believers or "bad" people. The fact that the artist adheres to a different worldview should not be one of them. The church ought to be first in line and the most vocal to praise the good, true, and beautiful wherever it appears, for all goodness, truth, and beauty ultimately points toward God.

What Makes Christian Art "Christian"?

The Christian arts and entertainment subculture is a strange phenomenon. For a religion whose namesake commissioned his disciples to "go into all the world" **(Mark 16:25)**, Christians have done much to distance ourselves from the wider culture. The secular/sacred divide in the arts has arguably never been as clear as it is today.

On the surface, the "Christian" art label (or the more contemporary—but equally murky— "faith-based" descriptor) is a convenient way for Christians to find art and entertainment that affirms our spiritual convictions and doesn't assault our moral standards. As Hollywood continues to fling filth and cram worldly ideologies into much of today's entertainment, there are clear benefits to a simple framework of sacred v. secular. After all, Christians are also called "to live a holy life" **(1 Thess. 4:7)**.

The question is *what makes Christian art "Christian"?*

The Artist's Faith?

The "Christian" label is an oddity that is unlike any other aesthetic category. For example, "Christian music" is the only musical category that is wholly classified by something other than musical style. Heavy metal, worship hymns, singer-songwriter folk tunes, and rap songs all exist side-by-side under the ambiguous label of "Christian," whereas Taylor Swift and Ariana Grande are unlikely to ever share a display shelf with Cannibal Corpse or Slipknot.

One obvious implication is that the unifying element of Christian art is the musicians' shared Christian faith. Yet, while the artist's faith is undoubtedly a factor, the great religious cathedral art that was painted by unbelieving artists demonstrates the shortcoming of the simplistic equation: "Christian art = art made by Christians."

People typically have more than just the artist's faith in mind when classifying art. I remember when a popular Christian rock band released the first song from their upcoming album. The debut track was a "party song" about the thrills of playing a rock concert. Listeners quickly bombarded the comments section with posts such as, "Aren't they a Christian band anymore?" and "I hope they have more Christian songs on the rest of the album." In other words, there is a general expectation that the *content* will somehow be "Christian."

Religious Content?

The content expected of Christian art is typically the depiction, declaration, or exploration of religious imagery, topics, or themes. Da Vinci's *The Last Supper*, the TV show *The Chosen*, and the music of *Hillsong* all fall into this category. While such art can be appreciated as entertainment, they wouldn't be out of place in a Sunday morning worship service. On most Christian radio stations, listeners are unlikely to hear lyrics that explore topics beyond God, worship, or faith. "Faith-based" art is thus art that deals explicitly with the topic of faith itself.

This limited range of permissible content has led to some almost comical lyrical gymnastics, such as the infamously vague pronoun "you," resulting in awkward songs that are either too romantic and mushy for God or too worshipful for a romantic crush. Also common is the statement, "We're not a Christian band. We're Christians *in* a band." The declaration is both an affirmation of the secular/sacred divide and a desperate attempt to break free from it.

The necessity of religious content also results in the unfortunate artistic homelessness of abstract painters, instrumental musicians, and dancers, who are thus excluded from creating "Christian" art unless they force a contrived spiritual meaning to their otherwise sensory work. While religious art is fittingly understood as being "Christian," it does not follow that all "Christian" art must be "religious." Indeed, if "religious content" is required, then not even God—the Divine Artist— passes the test, as there is nothing religious about a sunset or shooting star.

For the Glory of God

Perhaps the best solution to our question is not to clarify the label of "Christian art" but to question it. Rather than trying to cross the chasm between the secular and sacred, perhaps it is more fruitful to reconsider the necessity of that forced binary choice.

The Christian arts and entertainment subculture is, after all, a relatively recent development that was not ushered in until the CCM movement in the 1960s. For most of history, Christians viewed the matter quite differently. A pious musician such as Johann Sebastian Bach distinguished between religious music composed for the church and music written for a "secular" context, but there was no notion that one was any more "Christian" than the other. Rather, he declared, "The aim and final end of all music should be none other than the glory of God and the refreshment of the soul." In this, Bach provides a worthy goal to which Christians should aspire today.

The calling of Christian artists is not to make "Christian" art; it is to glorify God **(1 Cor. 10:31)**. We shouldn't focus on labeling all art "Christian" or "secular" but on affirming the good, true, and beautiful wherever we find it **(Phil. 4:8)**. Christianity is more than religious activity. As born-again Christians, we are a beautiful new creation whether we are singing "hallelujah" in church or fixing an old car in our garage **(2 Cor. 5:17)**.

Even the popular terminology frequently used in churches and schools of "faith integration" is somewhat flawed and misleading. Integration implies that art and Christian faith exist separately and must somehow be brought together or that art must be "baptized" with Christian content or evangelistic purposes to be relevant to the Christian faith. Yet, the lordship of Christ is over all of creation, and Christian artists should be unshackled and given the freedom to explore all of human experience through their art. The act of artistic creation itself can be a worshipful offering to our creator.

Labels exist because they are useful. There are certainly benefits to the "Christian art" label. But we must recognize that this categorization is merely a signpost and not a template. In doing so, Christians can focus less on forcing art to fit into tidy boxes and more on creatively using the full breadth of artistic possibility to glorify an infinite God.

The Christian Home as a Training Ground, not a "Safe Space"

Christians often meet the term "safe spaces" with mockery and derision. "These overly sensitive snowflake college kids need to learn to handle free speech and challenging ideas!" At the same time, there is also a widespread perception that university is a brutal gauntlet where Christian faith goes to die. The concern is not based on a myth. Statistically, as many as 60-70% of Christian young adults leave the church once they graduate from high school and start college.

Thus, there is a tension between the church's desire for young adults to live in a world that is an open forum for contrasting ideas and the understanding that many young Christians are proving unable to withstand this reality. Complicated problems rarely have simple solutions, and there is no one-size-fits-all answer here. Nevertheless, I suggest that if the church wants to raise up young adults that don't need "safe spaces" at college, then we must strive to give our children something more than safe spaces at home.

A Training Ground

In one sense, the family is (or should be) a safe space. The world is filled with evil and trials, and the home should be a refuge of love and unconditional support. But the home should not be a safe space in the sense that children are insulated from all alternative ideas and beliefs. Instead, it should be a purposeful training ground.

I have found myself asking this question: What am I preparing my children for?

As a father of 7-year-old twin boys, I realize (sometimes reluctantly) that I may have only eleven years left to be a daily, physical influence in their lives. When this blissful period comes to an end, I pray I will launch into the world two Christ-like young men who are ready to go into the hardest areas of culture and shine the light of Jesus. I must then ask the next question: What must I do *now* to prepare them for that calling?

There is a world of difference between a college student and an elementary pupil. But just having birthday parties doesn't produce wisdom. Children do not suddenly become discerning because they are handed a high school diploma. Discernment is taught.

Jesus told his followers, "I am sending you out like sheep among wolves. Therefore be as shrewd as snakes and as innocent as doves" **(Matthew 10:16)**.

Christians are called to be innocent and holy. We are also commanded to be shrewd, wise, and discerning. A Christian home should foster *both* callings. Unfortunately, in my experience—and according to the sobering statistics—we are often sending children who are innocent as doves but not shrewd as serpents into a world of wolves, and they are being devoured.

A "Worldly" Education

When it comes to Christian views on media and entertainment, there is often a hefty dose of concern that borders on sensationalism. The amount of persuasive power Christians frequently attribute to today's popular entertainment implies that if children so much as walk past a *Harry Potter* novel on a school library shelf, they will be dragged into a life in the occult. When I've reviewed movies, I've earned several ALLCAPS comments telling me that I had no right to claim the title of "Christian" if I dare to do anything other than angrily denounce every Hollywood film as demonic. Entertainment is evil, they argue, and Christians should have nothing to do with it whatsoever.

Stripped of the sensationalist expressions, I understand the valid concern. I have a PhD in aesthetics and culture and have researched the topic from every lens possible—philosophy, psychology, sociology, theology, etc.—and there is almost universal agreement that art and entertainment *do* impact people, often in subtle and unexpected ways (wherein lies the peril). Christians are foolish to underestimate the power of entertainment. Yet, overestimating it is also dangerous. The primary hazard in secular entertainment is not that it exists but that it is consumed uncritically. The issue is not just that Christian young adults are growing up in a culture permeated by such entertainment but that they never learn how to navigate and engage with it.

Paul wrote, "Do not conform to the pattern of this world" **(Romans 12:2)**. Many Christians use this admonition as a justification to pull out of culture and shelter children from its harmful influence. Yet, Paul follows the statement by writing, "But be transformed by the renewing of your mind. Then you will be able to test and approve what God's will is—his good, pleasing and perfect will." In other words, the path to nonconformity is not withdrawing from the world but changing the way we think so we are wise and discerning while living in it.

If exposure to an unbiblical worldview presented in an animated movie is enough to cause a child to reject biblical truth, then there has been a serious breakdown in discipleship. If the faith I have labored for years to instill in my children cannot withstand the occasional Disney film, then I'm more troubled by my own shortcomings than I am outraged at secular Hollywood. I desire to guard my children's hearts from impurity and moral filth, but I also want to train their minds to know how to discern God's truth from the world's lies.

To be clear, I'm not suggesting that every tragedy of a child leaving the faith can be traced to a failure in parenting or church discipleship. Satan is the father of lies, and sin is persuasive and seductive. Judas Iscariot was discipled by Jesus himself, and he was still destroyed by the lies of the world. My intention is not to cast blame but merely to examine what we as the church can do to best equip our young adults for the challenges ahead.

Protected But Prepared

The world is filled with dangerous and seductive messages, and isolation is not the answer. If the church wants to raise up faithful young adults who go boldly into the world, then we can ill-afford to squander their formative years sheltering them from it. If a college classroom is the first place a Christian becomes aware of contrasting worldviews and secular ideologies, then the church has failed to "give an answer to everyone who asks" for the hope that they have **(1 Peter 3:15)**. We may have provided a quiver full of answers but never allowed them to engage with the questions.

The church shouldn't be surprised when our young adults are unable to withstand intelligent, persuasive assaults on their faith in university when we didn't even trust their biblical foundation to withstand

We are not equipping our young adults for an existence hidden away in safe bunkers, but for a courageous life on a spiritual battlefield.

Frozen 2 a few years earlier. The ideal time to teach children how to navigate secular worldviews is when they are sitting beside us in the living room, not when they live hundreds of miles away in a college dorm.

Notably, when Christian exiles and nomads (those who abandon or drift away from their faith after high school) are surveyed about their spiritual wandering, the reasons they give for leaving the church are almost never related to movies or entertainment (which is not to suggest that such exposure did not also play a role). Rather, most respond that the church was simply not a safe place to ask questions, express doubts, or talk about important real-world issues.

They didn't leave because they were shown too much of the world but because they weren't exposed to enough of it. They were ready to engage with cultural issues and questions, but when they found no welcoming forum to do so in the church, they searched for those answers in the world.

Does a 10-year-old need to watch raunchy R-rated comedies filled with a barrage of profanity and gratuitous sex to understand what the world is really like? Of course not. In fact, adults shouldn't be watching that content either. Christians—both young and old— are called to be holy and to guard our hearts and minds from filth. Providing young people with a "worldly education" doesn't mean recklessly exposing them to things before they are ready. Parents ought to pray for wisdom when navigating these issues. But secular philosophies and worldviews are out in the world, and children must be prepared for them.

When Jesus prayed a final commissioning prayer over his disciples, he said, "My prayer is not that you take them out of the world but that you protect them from the evil one" **(John 17:15)**.

Christians should be careful about allowing the Evil One a foothold in their life. Parents should protect their children—but retreating from the world was never God's plan. After all, we are not equipping our young adults for an existence hidden away in safe bunkers, but for a courageous life on a spiritual battlefield.

It's Time for the Church to Unleash Its Artists

There was a time in history when Christians were at the forefront of the arts. That's not true today. Christians remain active in the arts. In fact, thanks to the development of a growing Christian subculture, it could be argued that Christians are more involved in the arts than ever. Yet, whereas most of art history must grant significant chapters to the role and influence of Christianity, a survey of the last century might not include any references to the church at all. What happened?

There are no easy answers. Significant cultural and societal changes have played a critical role. Christianity is no longer the cultural default, and churches no longer possess the political or financial power the Catholic Church once enjoyed. But these changes tell only part of the story. There has also been a mindset shift. Somewhere along the way, the church simply stopped viewing itself as a patron of the arts.

During a recent church service, a leader on stage championed the potential of the younger generations and expressed excitement at how God will use them to transform the country. Some would be called as pastors, others might be sent as missionaries, and still more would be raised up as Sunday school teachers and worship leaders. I pray all of that is true. May God continue to raise up young people to serve as faithful shepherds of God's people. At the same time, I found myself asking, "What about the artists?"

Left on the Fringe

There is a tendency for churches to think about the Christian mission exclusively within the framework of church service. It's common for congregations to lay hands on young adults and commission them into Christian ministry. After summer youth camps, church leadership often reports on how many teenagers became Christians and how many were called into

Christian ministry. Both are worthy of celebration, but the limited range of these spiritual responses leaves those *not* called into professional ministry feeling like second-string players or the supporting cast to the more important Christian callings.

A problem with this mindset is that the world will not be transformed by pastors. Not exclusively, at least. The church body is predominately composed of lay people. Of course, lay people need faithful leaders to disciple and guide them. The Bible is clear that church leaders have a unique and crucial calling. But their responsibility is to equip people to go into the world, spread the gospel, and make disciples. The reason God continues to call people into pastoral ministry is because he has a divine purpose for lay people, including the creative artists.

In the body of Christ, artists are sometimes viewed as eyelashes. They add beauty, but most people aren't sure what functional purpose they serve. There are amazingly talented and gifted creatives in church every week whose God-given artistic abilities are called upon only once a year for the Christmas program. There are musicians whose talents are rarely, if ever, heard outside the church walls. Visual artists are taken out of the storage closet whenever a new mural is needed for the kids' Sunday school room and then promptly returned.

God has entrusted the church with creative artists. Is it being a good steward of them?

Biblical Aesthetics

The church should support artists because a world without art and beauty is simply a worse place to live. At the same time, an artist's calling is not wholly unrelated to the church's mission. Creativity and art play an important role in the church's commission.

The Bible is a prime example. Scripture includes plenty of dynamic sermons, prophetic teaching, and deep theological and doctrinal discourse. It also contains large collections of poetry, compelling narratives, and captivating parables. Jesus preached sermons, but he also told stories and used visual symbols. In other words, the creative arts have always played an important role in the Christian movement.

Right-Brained Church

As actual science, the "right brain v. left brain" dichotomy is largely a myth. The human brain is far more complex than that. But as a metaphor, it is a helpful reminder that people are wired differently. God is not just Lord of the left-brained. He is Lord of all. The church needs preachers, apologists, and philosophers. It also needs artists.

Many artists are naturally sensitive to people's hurts and doubts and explore areas others dare not tread. Good artists are typically keen observers and listeners. It is unsurprising that even secular artists often adopt an identity as cultural "prophets." There is something innately religious and spiritual about the role of artists.

The church should empower artists not as a charity but because artists add value to the body of Christ.

Using Creatives v. Sending Creatives

When asked to identify the darkest and most "godless" area of today's culture, I suspect many Christians would point to the art and entertainment culture. The most effective way to combat that darkness isn't with perpetual boycotts and complaints. The answer is already sitting in the church pews. Darkness is merely the absence of light. The only way to dispel cultural darkness is to send lights into the darkest areas. It is time for the church to equip its artists to become beacons of light in a world lost in darkness.

5 Classic Novels That Every Christian Should Read

Classic literature is a deep well, offering more nourishing water than even the most dedicated bookworm can hope to drink in a single lifetime. It is also an area Christians often neglect. We are a people of the Book, but we have not always been a people of books. Yet, Christians who ignore great literature are depriving themselves of the indispensable wisdom passed down by some of the greatest minds in history. The advantage of classic literature is that it has been tested. The rivers of time have washed away the inconsequential and preserved the works of true genius. Many novels that were popular during their day are now entirely forgotten, while some that were overlooked have been vindicated.

Below is a list of five classic novels every Christian would benefit from reading. The list is far from exhaustive. For example, *The Brothers Karamazov*, the Russian classic by Fyodor Dostoevsky, is frequently cited as essential reading for Christians. Other literary masterpieces, such as Herman Melville's *Moby Dick*, are filled with thought-provoking and edifying truth. These books are worth reading—but they take effort. They are not as accessible to today's casual reader. Therefore, the five novels below are among

> Christians who ignore great literature are depriving themselves of the indispensable wisdom passed down by some of the greatest minds in history.

the best that Christians should read that they *may actually read*. So, without further ado…

1. Fahrenheit 451 — by Ray Bradbury

"You don't have to burn books to destroy a culture. Just get people to stop reading them."

Time has emphatically affirmed the genius of Bradbury's prophetic dystopian narrative. The story of a society that bans and systematically burns books remains as timely today as when it was published in 1953. The novel is often interpreted as championing physical books in the digital age, but that interpretation is a misunderstanding. *Fahrenheit 451* is less about the importance of physical books than about the indispensable value of knowledge. The power is in the words, not the ink and pages.

Christian readers can take note of the way the book's central message relates to Scripture. The society of "Book People" that emerges near the end of the story seeks to preserve knowledge by memorizing books, including books of the Bible. The novel remains a timely warning against the mind-numbing distraction of constant and ubiquitous media and entertainment, and it will challenge Christians to evaluate the importance of truth, knowledge, and Scripture.

2. The Lord of the Rings — J. R. R. Tolkien

"But in the end it's only a passing thing, this shadow; even darkness must pass."

All Christians should take at least one pilgrimage to Middle-earth during their lifetime. Tolkien once referred to *The Lord of the Rings* as a "fundamentally religious and Catholic work." Yet, whereas *The Chronicles of Narnia* (written by his dear friend C. S. Lewis) can be reduced to a game of "spot the Christian allegory and symbolism," there is no simplistic interpretation of Tolkien's masterpiece. The novel embodies Christian virtue rather than teaching it. It is more inspirational than didactic. In *Narnia*, the story is constructed like signposts to point toward Christian theology. In *The Lord of the Rings*, theology is the fertile soil out of which the story organically grows. The novel is far more complex than many critics in today's post-*Game of Thrones* culture might suggest. While adhering to a clear binary of cosmic good v. evil, nuance is evident in how the flawed characters operate in such a world.

Christian readers will be encouraged by the novel's elevation of Christian virtue, the inspirational depictions of characters heroically striving against the powers of evil, the role of divine sovereignty, and the many profound nuggets of wisdom sprinkled throughout. A literary journey through *The Lord of the Rings* is like a cleansing shower that washes away the dirt and grime of today's culture.

3. Great Expectations — Charles Dickens

"I have been bent and broken, but—I hope—into a better shape."

Dickens belongs in any conversation about history's greatest authors. He is worth reading for his mastery of language and immense wit. A Charles Dickens sentence is a work of art unto itself. Most readers, however, approach a novel primarily for its plot, and in this area Dickens delivers as well. Despite their age and cultural

context, his novels remain as timely and relevant as ever in their exploration of social justice, politics, power of the press, Christian virtue, and social relations. *A Tale of Two Cities* is his best-known work, *Bleak House* his greatest, and *David Copperfield* his most enjoyable, but *Great Expectations* is perhaps the best entry point for a first-time reader. One of only a handful of Dickens novels told from the first-person perspective, the book is a coming-of-age story about a boy named Pip as he develops a moral awareness and formulates a Christian worldview.

Christian readers will benefit from experiencing Pip's realization of his sinful nature, his seduction into pride, and his eventual humbling and maturation. Dickens' religious convictions do not manifest as overtly as is typical of much Christian fiction today, but Christian truth permeates *Great Expectations* from beginning to end.

4. The Pilgrim's Progress — John Bunyan

"Just as Christian came up to the Cross, his burden loosed from off his shoulders, ..."

The Pilgrim's Progress is one of the best-selling works of literature ever written, although its popularity seems to have waned in recent decades. Although allegory is a common genre in Christian fiction today—thanks in large part to the influence of C. S. Lewis—it was not so when Bunyan penned his great novel from a prison cell. In fact, Bunyan begins his book with an *apology* for deploying allegorical and fantastic elements to examine theological truth. Despite the author's concerns, the story has challenged and edified countless readers since it was written.

By today's standards, the allegorical tale may seem outdated (it was first published in 1678, after all!) and too "on-the-nose." Yet, the beauty of *Pilgrim's Progress* is in its outward simplicity and its ability to add tangible form to deep theological and spiritual truth. The patient Christian reader who embraces the older style will come away with new reflections and insights into the Christian life, salvation, and what it means to faithfully seek God.

5. Jane Eyre — Charlotte Brontë

"Life appears to me too short to be spent in nursing animosity or registering wrongs."

Jane Austen and the three Brontë sisters (Charlotte, Emily, and Anne) are often dismissed as being "for girls." During their lifetime, however, Austen published anonymously, and the Brontë sisters wrote under male pseudonyms, allowing their initial audiences to enjoy the books for their own merits without the baggage of simplistic labels. While Jane Austen remains more popular today, the Brontës wrote with more grit and perhaps appeal more to modern sensibilities. On the surface, Charlotte Brontë's *Jane Eyre* is a romance story, but it is far *more* than that. Similar in style and purpose to Dickens' *Great Expectations*, it is a coming-of-age tale (or a *Bildungsroman*, to use a fun literary term!) tracing Jane's physical, mental, moral, and spiritual growth from childhood to adulthood.

Christian readers—men and women alike—will be challenged by Jane's steadfast faithfulness and virtue. The power of the novel is not merely that Jane Eyre grows to embody a Christian worldview but that Charlotte Brontë convincingly demonstrates how such a world-view was developed. The adult Jane Eyre at the end of the novel is much changed from the child at its beginning. It is through the crucible of life that faith is grown and tested, and Christian readers will find their own faith challenged and strengthened alongside Jane Eyre.

5 More Classic Novels That Every Christian Should Read

Mark Twain once quipped, "A classic is something that everybody wants to have read and nobody wants to read." No doubt, bookshelves are filled with beautifully bound classic books that have never been cracked open. A book is a gorgeous sight to behold (and don't even get me started on that wonderful "book smell"), but what makes books valuable are the words they contain.

Earlier this year I wrote an article called *Five Classic Novels That Christians Should Read*. My purpose was simple: to share my love of classic literature. I anticipated it would be a niche article I enjoyed writing, but that it wouldn't find a wide audience. To my surprise (and delight), that article became one of the most popular ones we've ever published, with many people weighing in with their own personal recommendations. Bookworms truly are the best.

A Charles Dickens' novel is read against the backdrop of the political and social conditions of 19th-century England, but we don't read classic novels just to learn about history. Classic literature's value is that it transcends its setting and contains universal themes and edifying truth. Its less accessible packaging may require more work and patience than other books, but that is part of the charm. Classic novels entertain and enlighten, but they also require something in return. They ask us to slow down and open ourselves up to all they have to offer.

Here are five (more) classic books that Christians should read.

1. The Lion, the Witch, and the Wardrobe — C. S. Lewis

"The Stone Table was broken into two pieces by a great crack that ran down it from end to end; and there was no Aslan."

Every Christian should take at least one trip through the wardrobe into the fantastical land of Narnia. The younger the better, but Aslan welcomes readers of all ages. *The Chronicles of Narnia* is firmly engrained alongside *The Lord of the Rings* and *The Pilgrim's Progress* as one of the most beloved works of fiction in all of Christendom. The story is escapist fantasy at its best, filled with evil queens, magical creatures, anthropomorphic animals, and epic battles.

Christians can enjoy the novel for its captivating narrative and also for its rich theological underpinnings. Unlike the more embodied religious elements in Tolkien legendarium, there is an overtly evangelistic aspect to the Narnia stories. *The Lion, the Witch, and the Wardrobe* is not technically an allegory, since it lacks a one-to-one correlation. Rather, Lewis sought to "reimage the Gospel" by recasting it in vivid, fantastical imagery. Christian readers will experience a fresh sense of wonder and understanding of their faith, and some of the images—a roaring lion or a broken stone table—may remain with them as lifetime companions.

2. Pride and Prejudice — Jane Austen

"It is very often nothing but our own vanity that deceives us."

Jane Austen is perhaps the most famous and beloved female author in history, despite publishing anonymously during her lifetime. A stigma about Austen's stories is that they are merely mushy romances for girls. The Hollywoodization of the film adaptations is partially to blame for this image, as they fail to capture the satire and sharp wit in her work. To be clear, there is indeed plenty of romance to be found, with the basic plot of every novel involving musical chairs of which girl ends up with which boy (#TeamBingley). But her books have far more to offer than love stories. A clergyman's daughter, her writing exemplifies a pious Christian worldview and penetrating insight into social relationships.

Emma is her most hilarious and enjoyable work. *Mansfield Park* and *Persuasion* (published posthumously) feature more mature and virtuous heroines. But if you only read one Austen novel, it should be *Pride and Prejudice*, her most famous work. The manuscript was originally titled *First Impressions*, which is a succinct summation of the central theme. The story traces the moral growth of the various characters as they overcome their shortsighted assumptions and judgments of each other. Present-day Christian readers may not live in the same genteel, aristocratic British society as Elizabeth Bennett and Fitzwilliam Darcy, but the novel can help challenge and deconstruct our own pride and prejudices.

3. The Count of Monte Cristo — Alexandre Dumas

"Until the day when God shall deign to reveal the future to man, all human wisdom is summed up in these two words,-Wait and hope."

A classic revenge story (and a precursor to the Batman character), *The Count of Monte Cristo* weaves a complex narrative about a man named Edmond Dantès who escapes from a wrongful imprisonment and, with the help of a seemingly limitless fortune, slowly plots the downfall of the men responsible. While movie adaptations often render the story into a swashbuckling adventure tale, the novel has more in common with a Shakespearian tragedy. It's a slow-burn, methodical character study of the dehumanizing cost of anger, bitterness, and revenge. On a deeper level, the main theme is nothing less than the original sin of mankind—elevating ourselves into the place of God.

Edmond Dantès desires justice and comes to believe that he is acting as the hands of God. Dantès is the protagonist, but the uncomfortable tension at the heart of the book is that he isn't a hero. A key moment in the novel is when he realizes he has gone too far: "[H]e felt he had passed beyond the bounds of vengeance, and that he could no longer say, 'God is for and with me.'" Dumas' great novel explores the line between human justice and God's eternal and perfect justice, raising difficult questions without always providing easy answers. In an age when justice (or the lack of it) is a primary concern, *The Count of Monte Cristo* remains a relevant and timely cautionary tale.

4. Les Misérables — Victor Hugo

"Love is the foolishness of men, and the wisdom of God."

We're plunging into the deep end of the pool now. If you haven't read many classic books, Victor Hugo's masterpiece is not the most accessible starting point. An apt descriptor for the book is "abundance." The novel is exceptionally long. Like Leo Tolstoy's *War and Peace*, Hugo's ambition is greater than telling a straightforward narrative. He paints his sprawling canvas with elements of history, politics, art, and life in all its facets. Side tangents that go on for 30 or 40 pages can spark frustration. But the extensive tale is a tonic for our rapidly paced lives and shortening attention spans. By forgoing a simplistic narrative structure, the story almost forces readers to immerse themselves in the life and rhythm of the characters, thus more keenly experiencing wisdom and truth along the way.

Christian readers who take the daunting plunge will be inspired by how Christian virtue can ripple across history. *Les Misérables* is a generational story, unfolding over the course of many years and tracing the ways seemingly simple acts of forgiveness, grace, and compassion can change the trajectory of a life. Bishop Myriel—one of the most towering pillars of Christian faith in all of fiction—exits the story after the opening few chapters, but his profound influence is felt throughout the whole novel and echoes in the life and actions of Jean Valjean. *Les Misérables* is not for the faint of heart, but the hearts of those who read it will be stirred and compelled to a life of greater Christian charity.

5. Frankenstein — Mary Shelley

"Accursed creator! ...God, in pity, made man beautiful and alluring, after his own image; but my form is a filthy type of yours, more horrid even from the very resemblance."

Let's get this out of the way first: Frankenstein is the name of the scientist, not the monster. Mary Shelley's influential science-fiction novel bears little resemblance to the various movie adaptations. Although at times spooky and horrific, it is a deeply philosophical story. The monster spends more time monologuing about the meaning of life than it does terrorizing people (although it does that too). The book explores the relationship between creation and creator. As with many classic works of science fiction, the story exposes the disastrous consequences that arise when man attempts to climb the ladder of scientific advancement and reach for godhood.

Christian readers will be drawn to reflect on their relationship to their own creator whose image they bear. As a created being, the monster represents another Adam narrative—a parallel drawn by the creature itself—but with sinful man, rather than a loving God, as its creator. *Frankenstein* is a gospel story stripped of divine hope, a bleak picture in which sin begets sin in an endless and destructive cycle. The book also challenges Christians to reflect on the influence their actions can have. The innocent monster begins as a gentle, curious creature but develops into a sinister fiend largely due to the way it is treated and viewed by the world.

From Trending to Trendy: Loving People with More than Hashtags

Pop culture is both a mirror and an incubator. It reflects the prevailing ideologies, values, and passions of the world today, while also shaping the culture of tomorrow. The rich and famous in the entertainment industry are no more important than the average person, but they are certainly more visible, and there is immense power in that visibility. While some people dismiss the happenings in culture as merely the words and actions of the out-of-touch Hollywood elite, pop culture often reveals a deeper undercurrent of what is taking place in the world.

#MeToo & Time's Up

The #MeToo movement was born out of the concussive aftermath of the Harvey Weinstein scandal in 2017. While members of the Hollywood elite were recognized as the perpetrators of rampant sexual exploitation in the entertainment industry, it was also those within Hollywood who ignited the movement to fight the abuse.

Christians don't need to be aligned with an entertainer's voting record or opinions on hot-button issues to stand in solidarity against sexual abuse. The #MeToo movement was not a Hollywood issue; it was a human one.

Much has changed in culture since 2017, and a lot of positive progress has been gained (even if much work remains). Yet, with the benefit of hindsight, the movement has also exposed some shortcomings of viral, cultural crusades.

The Hollywood Reporter recently published an article detailing the rise and fall of the Time's Up organization. Despite name-recognition and good intentions at the forefront of the initial #MeToo wave, the group is now a "ghost organization":

"Instead of providing a voice for the voiceless, the organization ended up crumpling amid conflict-of-interest allegations and internal disagreements over its focus."

"Outside of pins being adorned to very fancy dresses on the red carpet, what came out of that organization?"

"Money and power took over everything, and their mission drifted into seeing how many powerful people they could get at a lunch table."

What went wrong?

From Trending to Trendy

The problem with trending movements is that they can quickly become trendy movements. Viral hashtags and catchy slogans can be a double-edged sword. They spread quickly but can also usurp the issue itself. They become an easy way for people to stand up and be counted, while requiring little action. In a sense, the hashtags and slogans used to popularize a movement often become a movement unto themselves.

I remember when everyone posted black boxes on their Instagram accounts, but I can't recall what cause triggered it. I recall when people filmed themselves being dunked with ice water. The purpose was to raise awareness for a disease, but most people probably couldn't identify which one. Instead, the movement became about trying to raise the ante with increasingly viral videos. These movements—and many others—quickly went from people spreading awareness about an important issue to people spreading awareness about what important issues they support. It became about *being activists* rather than activism.

Words & Action

Jesus constantly confronted this sort of behavior: "Why do you call me, 'Lord, Lord,' and do not do what I say?" **(Luke 6:46)**. When he asked Peter three times if he loved him, Peter became exasperated and insisted that he did. Jesus responded, "Feed my lambs," "Shepherd my sheep," and "Feed my sheep" **(John 21)**.

The demise of the Time's Up organization is not something to celebrate, nor is it an indication that the people involved don't care about sexual abuse. But it's a reminder that loving people and seeking justice for them is messier and more complicated than catchy slogans or social media posts. Hashtags and viral trends of solidarity are powerful tools to distill important issues into simple messages, but the issues themselves are rarely simplistic. Hashtags don't change the world. Hashtags inspire and mobilize people to make a difference in the culture around them as God works in and through them.

The love of Christ should compel the church to more than a trendy expression of our faith **(2 Corinthians 5:14)**. It is easy to post a pretty Bible verse graphic on Instagram but more demanding to live in the truth of that scripture in the real world. It feels good to declare, "There's no judgment here," but harder to stop making sweeping judgments about people who think, act, or vote differently. In short, the world doesn't need Christians just to stand up and be counted. It needs Christians to be the active hands and feet of Jesus, loving people and shining light in a dark world.

REVIEWS

Black Panther: Wakanda Forever

An emotional and meaningful film that struggles not to buckle under its own weight, succeeding more as a cultural moment than as an exciting or cohesive story.

Black Panther: Wakanda Forever would have been one of the year's most anticipated films under any circumstances, but the tragic death of actor Chadwick Boseman adds an inseparable dimension. The movie is by far the weightiest and most emotional Marvel film to date, a meaningful—sometimes beautiful—tribute to its beloved actor and cherished character. At the same time, it doesn't always soar as high as a compelling or cohesive story. *Wakanda Forever* is far from a bad movie. In fact, it has excellent moments. But it's a busy film that often buckles under its own weight.

The movie handles the loss of its lead actor/character as well as is feasibly possible. His presence is felt from start to finish, including an adjusted opening title card that essentially functions as a moment of silence. There is clear synergy between reality and fiction. For both the characters and the audience, the story unfolds almost like a guided process of cathartic mourning.

A byproduct of a Black Panther film without the Black Panther is that it is more of an ensemble story. Letitia Wright as Shuri takes a central role and gives a superb performance. Angela Bassett is also great as a grieving mother, and Lupita Nyong'o is always a welcome presence (despite limited screentime). Another standout is the newly introduced character of Namor, who is easily one of the most compelling villains in the MCU canon. Actor Tenoch Huerta doesn't necessarily have the magnetic charisma to steal or command many scenes, but the character is so well developed that he is truly a character in his own right, not just a necessary foil for the heroes.

Despite its emotional earnestness, not everything in *Wakanda Forever* works. Thematically, the film is razor-focused and unified. Narratively, however, it is jumbled and convoluted. The story unfolds as a collection of scenes and moments that don't always flow. The story constantly jumps to new locations and introduces new characters (that don't add much) to an already crowded cast. Even when the film hits the middle of its lengthy runtime, it still feels like it's just revving its engine.

Although director Ryan Coogler's fingerprints are evident, the movie lacks the kinetic energy of the thrilling first *Black Panther* film. Whereas *Black Panther* popped with vibrant color and visceral action, its sequel feels noticeably muted. One reason is that the story is more somber, but it is also simply the result of some uninspiring storytelling decisions. *Wakanda Forever* is plot heavy and filled with a barrage of exposition. The story is emotional, but never all that fun or exciting. It may be a satisfying meditation on a specific cultural moment, but there is little to compel audiences to rewatch it, and it will be interesting to see how the film is viewed in the future.

In the end, *Wakanda Forever* is a unique film with a worthy message. There is lots to appreciate, and there are flashes of brilliance, but it is largely held back by a jumbled and unexciting story. It's an excellent tribute to both Chadwick Boseman and the Black Panther character, but not the masterful sequel to *Black Panther* some may expect.

On the Surface: For Consideration

Profanity
A handful of minor profanities (mainly "sh—").

Violence
Standard, mostly bloodless MCU action. Several times, music (a siren's call) puts characters in a trance and compels them to toss themselves into the ocean (and presumably drown).

Sexuality
In one brief scene, a woman kisses another woman on the head and calls her, "my love," with seemingly romantic undertones, although the nature of their relationship is not explicitly stated.

Other
Pagan spirituality plays a central role in the story. Characters pray to "the gods" or to the specific god of their people. Several funeral rituals are performed. There is frequent talk about characters joining their ancestors or having their ancestors watch over them. A ritual transports a character to the "ancestral plane."

Beneath The Surface: Engage The Film

Overcoming Grief and Finding Faith

From start to finish, *Wakanda Forever* is an exploration of grief. It asks difficult questions, such as, "How do we move on from tragedy?" and "How does loss shape us, for better or worse?" A strength of the film is that it allows its characters to confront these questions with raw, honest emotion. The Bible says there is "a time to cry and a time to laugh. A time to grieve and a time to dance" **(Ecclesiastes 3:4)**. Grieving is a natural reality. The characters respond to the tragic loss of T'Challa in different ways, and the film never seems to judge them or suggest that one response is better than the others. While the story cautions against allowing grief to become all-consuming or lead to destructive anger, it also serves as a reminder that there is no one path to healing.

In the film, grief also drives characters toward faith and spirituality. While this spirituality is not presented in a strictly biblical sense (see Content to Consider above), the overarching theme is nevertheless powerful. The movie begins with a voiceover of a prayer that ultimately goes unanswered, resulting in a spiritual journey for the grieving character. There is a fascinating conversation between the queen and Shuri, as the queen attempts to guide her daughter through a religious ritual to find peace and feel her brother's presence. Scientifically minded Shuri dismisses the advice, asserting that the feeling is merely a mental construct, not real. Her mother responds by challenging Shuri as to what "mental construct" her own brain is making and whether it is bringing her peace.

Shuri retreats from her grief into science and technology but can't find peace in her more naturalistic worldview. On several occasions, she questions or lashes out against spiritual things and their futility to prevent her brother from dying. By the end of the film, however, she is on a path toward faith, reaching a satisfying conclusion that bookends the opening scene. While the film's conception of faith and spirituality doesn't reflect biblical Christianity, the general theme is consistent with the comforting invitation by Jesus, "Come to me, all you who are weary and burdened, and I will give you rest" **(Matthew 11:28)**.

Rings of Power (Season 1)

While not the flawless masterpiece some viewers desired, *The Rings of Power* is a well-crafted, visually beautiful, and thematically rich return to Middle-earth.

Faster than a hobbit leaving the Shire on a new adventure, Amazon's highly anticipated *Lord of the Rings* prequel has wrapped its first season. The show came with almost impossibly lofty expectations. In the end, despite some moments of flawed execution and script-writing, the first season of *The Rings of Power* was an immersive, compelling, and highly satisfying return to Middle-earth.

Whether *The Rings of Power* is "faithful" to Tolkien may depend on how you define terms. If the expectation is a dramatized *Silmarillion* wiki page, the show will surely disappoint. I understand the frustration some "purists" have toward the many changes to the established lore of Tolkien's legendarium. But I was less worried about a one-to-one reproduction of the expansive lore than that the show captures the "spirit" of Tolkien (which I know is subjective). In the eyes of this Tolkien-obsessed reviewer, it succeeds. *The Rings of Power* feels like Middle-earth.

Part of the "spirit" of Tolkien is the tone. In an era in which the fantasy genre is largely dominated by gritty realism and moral ambiguity, *The Rings of Power* is unabashedly hopeful and earnest. While other fantasy shows, such as *Game of Thrones*, emphasize the darkness in the heart of every person, *The Rings of Power* showcases that deep down there is goodness in the world that can pierce the gloom. It was refreshing to watch a show in which characters are quick to trust and friendships are not shaken by every new conflict or misunderstanding.

The Rings of Power is easily one of the best-looking television shows ever made, with visuals that hold up to or even surpass the quality of most theatrical movies this year. Some of the shots and frames are stunning, with a painting-like aesthetic. The exquisite visuals are supported by a superb musical score by Bear McCreary.

The show is not without issues. Outside the ire of the "lore purists," perhaps the most frequent criticism is that the pacing is too slow. The critique is valid. A byproduct of its ambitious scope and attempt to balance such a large ensemble cast is that the show doesn't always have a sense of forward motion or energy.

It can feel slow, even if significant plot developments are happening. One reason for its sluggishness is that characters frequently stand around and talk to each other about their motivations rather than demonstrating them through action. To a degree, this approach is more consistent with Tolkien's own storytelling sensibilities than was Peter Jackson's action-heavy film trilogy. In the book, the exposition-heavy Council of Elrond goes on for almost 40 pages, while the epic battle at Helm's Deep occupies just a few. To appeal to and engage modern audiences, however, the show would do well to trust that its audience can follow the plot and character developments without having the exposition dumped into another stoic dialogue.

I typically avoid assigning a reductionist numerical rating to shows or movies, but if forced to do so at the tip of a Morgul blade, I would place season one somewhere in the 7.5 to 8.0 range. The show was not always as compelling as the source material warrants, and there are areas in which it is clearly still finding its legs. It may not be the flawless masterpiece many people desired, but it is nevertheless a triumph. The show offers a well-crafted, visually beautiful, thematically rich return to Middle-earth and an intriguing start to what promises to be a great adventure.

On the Surface: For Consideration

Profanity
None. At one point, a character is interrupted just as he is about to swear.

Violence
The show is more violent and bloody than Peter Jackson's film trilogy. Characters have their stomachs mauled by creatures; blood spurts and limbs are severed during battle scenes; blood gushes profusely from both human and orc wounds; the camera lingers as swords pierce bodies.

Sexuality
None.

Other

The show may be frightening for younger viewers. The orcs are menacing, and some of the imagery—such as the aftermath of a battle or disaster—is intense and (intentionally) grim.

Beneath The Surface: Engage The Film

Find the Light

A major theme is about finding the light in a world of increasing darkness. As with *The Lord of the Rings*, the theme is more nuanced than a simplistic good v. evil. The show does not divide good and evil as clearly among the races (the elves are brought down from their lofty pedestal, and even the orcs are given some humanity). The show establishes that good and evil are absolutes, but each individual must strive to "find the light," as one character says.

Legacies & The Past

There is a repeated motif about the tension between the past and the future. In the early episodes, two quotes by different characters are juxtaposed: "The past is with us all," and "The past is gone. Let it die." Characters such as Galadriel and Halbrand confront this tension on an individual level, as Galadriel declares to Halbrand, "Let us redeem both of our bloodlines."

The theme is also explored on a wider, more communal level. Durin, the dwarven prince, and Nori, the inquisitive Harfoot, push against the established traditions of their people. One of the show's strengths is that it is willing to let its characters work through these thorny questions without providing definitive or simple answers.

Faith & Providence

Galadriel exhorts the queen regent of Númenor, "Choose not the path of fear, but that of faith." Religious imagery and themes are laden throughout the show, particularly relating to faith and trust in a higher design. Nori believes that she was *meant* to find the Stranger, and Galadriel declares that her introduction to Halbrand "was no chance meeting." There is a sense that everything happens for a reason. This faith in providence is repeatedly tested. In one particularly rich scene, Galadriel and Theo engage in the classical philosophical problem of evil. She remains steadfast in her belief in providence, while Theo questions how he can trust the hand of providence when he is confronted with the ruined wasteland of his home.

Thor: Love and Thunder

While hilarious at times and exploring some interesting themes surrounding faith and religion, the film's endless barrage of gags becomes wearisome, and the once-fresh "rock n' roll comedy" vibe is starting to feel tired and overdone.

Everybody's favorite space Viking is back, traveling through the Bifrost and into theaters for the latest entry in the Marvel Cinematic Universe. The God of Thunder is no longer the mighty avenger he once was, and he must undergo much soul searching to rediscover his purpose. The same is not true of *Thor: Love and Thunder* as a film, which has a clear identity and vision. Whether that identity is a pleasant one is up for discussion.

Viewers' enjoyment of *Thor: Love and Thunder* will largely depend on how they feel about director Taika Waititi's storytelling sensibilities. For the most part, I liked the comical, irreverent vibe Waititi introduced in *Thor: Ragnarok* (2017). That quirky sense of humor has now been cranked to eleven. At times, it works. There are some legitimately hilarious moments, including one involving two giant, magical goats and an ongoing gag about Thor's axe feeling jealous of his original hammer, Mjolnir. On the other hand, the unrelenting attempts at bizarre comedy become tiresome at times. Even more so than he did in *Ragnarok*, in this film Waititi goes for the joke every time. As a result, it often feels like a series of hit-or-miss SNL sketches rather than a unified film, with the story always in service of the gags rather than the jokes flowing organically out of the narrative.

Chris Hemsworth is as charismatic (and chiseled) as ever as Thor. But his character's humor has now been stretched to the point of being cartoonish, which reduces the thunderous superhero to a bumbling buffoon and undercuts his more serious moments. And Hemsworth is not the only Thor taking to the skies this time. Much of the buzz surrounding the film has stemmed from the surprising return of Natalie Portman, who appears not only as Jane Foster but also as Mighty Thor. The mechanics of her return is a bit clumsy, but Portman adds an interesting dynamic and is responsible for most of the film's heart.

The highlight of the movie is Christian Bale as the villainous Gorr the God Butcher. His character is treated with a horror tone (more chilling than anything in the recent horror-inspired Doctor Strange film), which provides a stark contrast to the movie's otherwise bright, bubblegum aesthetic. He is used sparingly, but his motivations are among the most believable of any MCU villain (more on that below).

Like the recent *Doctor Strange in the Multiverse of Madness*, this latest Thor adventure offers little to elevate it beyond the lower tier of the MCU. It's not a great movie, despite some enjoyable moments. There are flashes of creative brilliance, such as the superb cinematography and aesthetic of the Shadow Realm. But the vibe that felt fresh in 2017, with offbeat humor and action synced up with nostalgic rock music, is starting to become tired and overdone. The noisy barrage of gags left me worn out rather than energized.

On the Surface: For Consideration

Profanity

A fair number of mild profanities (mostly sh—).

Violence

Typical Marvel violence, almost entirely directed toward inhuman creatures. Shadowy monsters get dismembered in a variety of ways, with some creature gore visible.

Sexuality

Thor is briefly shown naked from behind. There is a repeated gag about a gathering of gods planning an orgy. An inhuman character shares about how his species procreates through a mating ritual involving two males ("my two dads"), which is shown later in the movie (the actual mating ritual is not depicted, but the two male characters are). A character's bisexuality is never overtly stated but is clearly demonstrated throughout. She is shown lusting after Thor, but she also recalls a former girlfriend and gives another female a flirtatious kiss on the hand.

Beneath The Surface: Engage The Film

Problem of Pain

Despite being a relatively fluffy and lightweight film, the story presents several interesting concepts with which Christians can engage. At the core of the story is an exploration of the classic problem of pain ("If God is all loving and all powerful, then why is there so much evil and suffering in the world?"). Gorr is introduced as deeply religious. He prays to his god to save his daughter's life, but she dies anyway. He becomes a broken man who has lost his faith in the benevolence of the divine, and he channels all his anger toward the gods.

Throughout the film, Gorr is frequently contrasted with Jane Foster. Both characters are grieving and struggling to accept the pain in their lives. While the hurt drives Gorr away from faith, it drives Jane—a woman of science—toward it. The film offers two vastly different perspectives on reality. One character sees pain as a curse from petty and vengeful gods, whereas the other finds love and meaning amid her suffering. The problem of pain is obviously far too complex and nuanced for a superhero movie to explore in much depth, and *Love and Thunder* doesn't give answers in a clear Christian sense. But the overall message is that pain and suffering are a part of being human. The same potential for love to hurt is also what makes it so satisfying and desirable. Christians can reflect on how their circumstances can shape their relationship with God, for better or worse.

Religion

Thor is a god from Norse mythology, so there has always been a religious dimension to his films, but religion has never played as central of a part as it does in *Love and Thunder.* There are various ways to approach these religious elements, and Christian viewers will likely have varying attitudes toward it. At no point does the religion in the movie reflect a Christian worldview (nor should anyone expect it to). Instead, the film presents all the gods from classical Roman and Greek mythology, as well as some newly invented ones, as real. Overall, the gods are depicted with a tone of mockery. They are selfish and petty egomaniacs. In this sense, *Love and Thunder* might be perceived as anti-religion.

At the same time, the unfavorable characterization of these gods is true to classical mythology. Zeus and the lesser gods were malicious and petty. In fact, the deities are essentially just superpowered individuals, rather than gods in a divine sense. Throughout the film, there is a feeling that a more mysterious divinity exists out there in the universe that is different from the other "gods." Rather than anti-religion, the film may be interpreted as deriding false religion. The movie takes fictional characters from mythology and treats them as fictional characters without applying the same treatment to the biblical God (ex. Jesus does not appear in the meeting of these deities, although there is a reference to a "God of Carpentry," which certainly leaves the door open as a possible reference to him). Christians can reflect on the loving character of the one true God by contrasting him with the self-serving nature of the false gods.

The Batman

A relentlessly dark tone, fresh and captivating aesthetic, and nuanced story work together for one of the best comic book movies in years.

The Bat Signal is shining, and the Batman is driving his flame-spouting new Batmobile back into movie theaters to answer the call. I'm a simple man. I hear that a new Batman movie is coming, and I get excited. Still, I had some questions. Do we really need another Batman? Will director Matt Reeves bring anything fresh to the character? Can Robert Pattinson, that sparkly vampire from *Twilight*, play a convincing Batman? The answer to all those questions is an emphatic yes.

The Batman is one of the best comic-book films in years. I'm not a big proponent of the comparison game. I prefer to evaluate a movie on its own merits rather than in contrast to other films. But while *The Batman* may lack some of the crowd-pleasing, high-spectacle, blockbuster re-watchability of Christopher Nolan's *Dark Knight Trilogy*, it is on that same lofty level.

The film has a clear vision and identity. *The Batman* is unrelentingly grim, rarely punctuating its melancholy tone with humor (although Colin Farrell's unrecognizable turn as The Penguin is good for some scene-stealing moments and laughs). The dark film squeezes as much juice out of its PG-13 rating as possible, landing somewhere between *The Dark Knight* and 2019's *Joker*. Some audiences, particularly Christian viewers, may understandably find fault with this brutal and grim identity. This version of the Batman character won't be for everyone. However, just as not every song needs to be a catchy singalong, not every superhero film must be bright or hopeful. *The Batman* character has always been a compelling vehicle to explore darker themes, and The Batman succeeds in doing that.

The film is long and moody, but that is not to suggest that it is slow or lacks gripping action. A nighttime car chase scene is edge-of-the-seat thrilling, with superb sound design that makes you feel the action as much as see it. While it has its fair share of good ol' fashioned goon-pounding, *The Batman* is more of a psychological thriller than an action movie. It is a testament to the strength of the script and pacing that the film maintains a near-constant level of tension despite its three-hour runtime.

Robert Pattinson is well suited (sorry) for the role as a young, mopey, and angry Batman. He is also almost exclusively *Batman*, with surprisingly sparse appearances as an unmasked Bruce Wayne. In fact, he might have more screen time in the batsuit than Christopher Bale did in the entire *Dark Knight Trilogy* combined. This is very much a Batman story. Zoë Kravitz is also well cast as Catwoman (or is she "purrfectly" cast?), even if her involvement in the action sometimes felt too convenient. Similarly, the romantic story beats felt abrupt and plot driven rather than earned, but that is a fault with the script and not Kravitz's performance. Arguably the star of *The Batman* is Gotham City itself. The corrupt cesspool of a city has never looked better, managing to feel grounded and believable but wholly fantastical and dystopian.

This movie is also perhaps the most socially conscious Batman film. You do not need to look too long or hard to draw real-world parallels. It touches on topics of conspiracy theories, racial tensions, corrupt cops, white supremacy, youth violence, toxic politics, and more. Time will tell whether this is a sticking point or not. While I noticed the inspirations, I was not bothered or distracted by them. These contemporary elements felt more like a way to ground the fantasy in familiar realism than an attempt to preach any particular agenda.

In the end, separating this version of Batman from the more supernatural DCEU and allowing the movie to fully embrace its dark, more grounded identity proved to be an inspired decision. I don't know if it's "the best Batman movie ever made," but it is certainly one of the freshest

On the Surface: For Consideration

Profanity

1 F-bomb, frequent other profanities, and repeated uses of the Lord's name in vain ("J— C—", "C—").

Sexuality

A woman is briefly shown in her underwear. A stripper is shown pole-dancing in the background of a club (she is blurry and not clearly visible). Prostitution is strongly implied. A lesbian relationship and a bi-sexual character are also clearly present, even if not directly depicted or affirmed.

Violence

Several characters are killed in violent ways. The violence is mostly implied rather than shown, but it is still unsettling.

Beneath The Surface: Engage The Film

Vengeance and Justice

When a city thug asks Batman his identity, Batman growls, "I'm vengeance." Batman then puts his words to action by beating the goon to a pulp. Although it is not explained in the film, it is implied that "The Vengeance" is the name adopted by Bruce Wayne for his vigilante persona and "The Batman" is merely the moniker others have given him. The name is fitting, as

one of the central themes is an exploration of vengeance in relation to justice.

When the movie begins, Bruce Wayne is two years into the Batman gig. He is not motivated by justice as much as by vengeance. In one scene, he knocks down a goon and then proceeds to pound him again and again, unleashing a violent fury of rage. In a visceral way, the moment highlights that Batman's desire is not just about cleaning up the city; it's also about punishing it. He wants to make Gotham pay for the pain he has experienced. The tension between Batman's selfless heroism and selfish vengeance is at the heart of the film and brings to mind Romans 12:17-19 and the truth that final vengeance belongs to God alone. In the end, vengeance serves no one.

Masks and Identity

A valid criticism of *The Batman* is that there is not much character development. While that may or may not be an issue on a narrative level, it works thematically. Batman is more of a symbol than a person. Bruce Wayne has been wholly consumed by the Batman. Arguably no Batman film has ever better depicted the physical and mental toll of being Batman.

Both Batman and the Riddler spend most of the film masked. The movie's tagline is "unmask the truth," but its central question is whether the masks conceal their true identity or reveal it. What is the difference between the two masked men?

The Dark Knight explored this theme through the relationship between Batman and *Joker*. Yet as great as that film is, it never convincingly demonstrated that the same chaos the Joker embodies also lives inside Batman. In *The Batman*, the similarity between Batman and *Riddler* is more clearly apparent. Bruce Wayne comes to realize that it is easier to crusade against the evils of the world than it is to look into the mirror and see the evil in his own heart or past. "You're a part of this too," the Riddler rightly sneers. Ultimately, the Batman must aspire to be more than an angry man in a mask.

Top Gun: Maverick

One of the best films of the year. An exhilarating sequel that delivers blockbuster cinema at its finest.

Do you feel the need? The need for speed? If so, you're in luck! At long last, this eagerly anticipated—and long delayed—sequel is flying into movie theaters, arriving a staggering 36 years after the original *Top Gun* (1986). Is it worth the wait? Absolutely! *Top Gun: Maverick* is superb, and it is easily one of the best movies of the year.

I loved almost everything about this film. In an age in which many people are quick to declare, "The future is streaming," *Top Gun: Maverick* is the quintessential theatrical experience and blockbuster cinema at its finest. The story picks up years after the events of the original film. Tom Cruise's Pete "Maverick" Mitchell is called back to the Top Gun flight school to train an elite batch of young pilots for a critical, seemingly impossible mission (good thing Mr. Cruise knows a thing or two about impossible missions).

The main attraction for a Top Gun movie is to watch cool fighter jets do cool things, and *Top Gun: Maverick* fully understands the assignment. The aerial scenes are phenomenal. I watched the film in a large Dolby theater, and the seats were rumbling as the jet engines roared to life. The flight scenes are felt as much as they are seen. Most of the aerial scenes actually occur as training exercises, with the only real combat occurring during the climactic mission at the end. Nevertheless, the film maintains unrelenting tension. And by the time that final mission arrives, the entire audience was holding our collective breath.

Top Gun: Maverick is not just about planes. One of the primary plot points is an emphasis on "the man inside the box." The new group of young pilots hold their own, even if none are developed with much depth and remain fairly one-dimensional (the "cocky" one, the "awkward" one, etc.). Only Miles Teller's "Rooster," the son of "Goose" from the original film, is given much to do. But the movie is called *Top Gun: Maverick*, not Top Gun: Next Generation. The film is very much a Tom Cruise-centric film, as he once again proves that he remains one of the few true "movie stars" in Hollywood.

At times, this sequel lays the nostalgia on thick with call-backs and familiar songs and locations from the original film. Yet the nostalgic elements never feel cheap; they serve the plot rather than becoming the plot. *Top Gun: Maverick* has a story worth telling and pushes all the right buttons when delivering it. My only complaint is that the theme song will now be stuck in my head indefinitely.

On the Surface: For Consideration

Profanity
1 prominent F-bomb and frequent other profanities (mostly sh—).

Sexuality
One implied (but not depicted) sexual encounter.

Violence
None. Fighter planes are shot from the sky and explode, but no blood or death is depicted.

Beneath The Surface: Engage The Film

Inspiring the Next Generation
The main narrative tension in the film is Maverick's transition from hot-shot pilot to flight instructor. He is clearly a superior pilot but struggles to equip the students. At one point during an emotional scene with Iceman (Val Kilmer), Maverick says, "A fighter pilot is *who* I am, not *what* I am. But how do I teach them that?"

Ultimately, he learns that he can't just tell them; he must *show* them. He had been lecturing them for weeks and running them through drills, but morale is low and the students are unable to complete the simulated mission. One of the film's best moments is when Maverick gets into a plane and shows them it can be done. By showing rather than telling, he inspires them to achieve more than they thought possible.

Maverick ends up with a prominent and active role in the mission, which may seem to undercut the theme of inspiring the next generation, but I think it actually offers a better and wiser approach. The story is not about "passing the baton" as much as it is about striving together side by side. It brings to mind the relationship between Paul and Timothy: "We sent Timothy, who is our brother and co-worker in God's service in spreading the gospel of Christ, to strengthen and encourage you in your faith" **(1 Thessalonians 3:2)**.

Another stand-out moment is a scene in which the pilots play football on the beach (a clear call-back to the Iconic scene in the original film). In the beginning, Maverick is right in the action with the young pilots. But eventually he exits to sit on the sidelines, observe, and let the young pilots play amongst themselves. The subtle moment provides a visual metaphor for a generational church where the young respect the wisdom of the older generations, the old leave space for the young, and all are united by a shared gospel mission.

About the Author

Daniel Blackaby

Daniel holds a PhD in "Christianity and the Arts" and a ThM in "Apologetics, Philosophy, and Worldview" from The Southern Baptist Theological Seminary. He is the author/co-author of multiple books, including the YA Fantasy trilogy "The Lost City Chronicles." He speaks in churches and schools across the country on the topics of Christian worldview, apologetics, creative writing, and the Arts.

www.ingramcontent.com/pod-product-compliance
Lightning Source LLC
Chambersburg PA
CBHW060944040426
42445CB00011B/993